# 150 Years on Pyrmont Peninsula

The Catholic Community of Saint Bede 1867–2017

C F Fowler

Journal Editor: James Franklin

ISSN: 0084-7259

**Contact**

General Correspondence, including membership applications and renewals, should be addressed to

The Secretary

ACHS

PO Box A621

Sydney South, NSW, 1235

Enquiries may also be directed to:

secretaryachs@gmail.com

**Executive members of the Society**
**President:**
Dr John Carmody
**Vice Presidents:**
Prof James Franklin
Mr Geoffrey Hogan
**Secretary:**
Ms Helen Scanlon
**Treasurer:**
Dr Lesley Hughes
**ACHS Chaplain:**
Sr Helen Simpson

**Cover image:** from the cover of *Armour of Light, The Stained Glass Windows of St James' Church, Forest Lodge*, book review on page 248

*Journal of the Australian Catholic Historical Society*

vol 37 (2) 2016

## Contents

Colin Fowler, Anti-Catholic polemic at the origins of Australia's first Catholic newspaper ... 147

Jeff Kildea, Killing conscription: the Easter Rising and Irish Catholic attitudes to the conscription debates in Australia, 1916-1917 ... 161

Anne Thoeming, Dr Herbert Michael ("Paddy") Moran: Catholic disruptor and contributor to Australian social history ... 181

Youssef Taouk, The Pope's Peace Note of 1917: The British response ... 193

Anne-Maree Whitaker, Linda Kearns and Kathleen Barry fundraising tour 1924-5 ... 208

Wanda Skowronska, Psychology's beginnings in Australia and some early Catholic responses ... 212

John de Luca, Golden jubilee of ordination homily ... 220

Moira O'Sullivan, A memoir of the value of religious life for one individual ... 228

Book review: Colin Fowler, *150 Years on Pyrmont Peninsula: The Catholic Community of Saint Bede 1867–2017*, reviewed by Damian Gleeson ... 241

Book review: Gerard Henderson, *Santamaria: A most unusual man*, reviewed by James Franklin ... 243

Book review: Wayne Hudson, *Australian Religious Thought*, reviewed by James Franklin ... 245

Book review: Anne Wark, *Armour of Light: The stained glass windows of St James' Church, Forest Lodge*, reviewed by Max Solling ... 248

Book review: Joan McBride, *When We Are Weak Then We Are Strong: A History of the Marist Sisters in Australia, 1907-1984*, reviewed by Robyn Dunlop ... 250

Book review: Julie Thorpe, *Aquinas Academy 1945-2015: A very personal Australian story*, reviewed by Xavier Symons ... 253

Book review: Kevin Peoples, *Santamaria's Salesman*, reviewed by Gregory Melleuish ... 256

Book review: Edmund Campion, *Swifty*, reviewed by Helen Scanlon ... 259

Book review: Leonard Faulkner, *A Listening Ministry*, reviewed by Michael Costigan ... 261

Book review: Hugh Mackay, *Beyond Belief*, reviewed by Roy Williams ... 266

## Anti-Catholic polemic at the origins of Australia's first Catholic newspaper

### Colin Fowler*

1838 was a significant year for the progress of the Catholic community in Australia. The previous year Bishop John Bede Polding had sent his Vicar General, William Bernard Ullathorne, to Europe on a recruiting mission. He was extraordinarily successful, not in recruiting English Benedictines as Polding had hoped, but in signing up Irish diocesan clergy for the mission. During 1838, from February to December, a total of thirteen Irish priests arrived in Sydney. The *Sydney Gazette* had given a sour announcement of the July arrivals:

*William Augustine Duncan (1811-1885), by unknown photographer. NLA reference number: nla.obj-138018450*

> The Cecilia, from London, on Sunday last, has brought us eight additional Irish Roman Catholic Priests, being the 'first-fruits' of Dr Ullathorne's pamphlet, at a cost to the Colony, which he has calumniated and injured of only £1,200! - We expect shortly to see the Colony swarming with these adventurous spirits, if, as in the present instance our emigration fund is to be taxed with the payment of £150 to each Priest to defray the expense of his passage here, and to give the gentleman an 'out-fit', a system of robbery of which we shall say more on an early day.[1]

As the priests arrived Polding wasted no time in dispersing them throughout

---

*Colin Fowler is a member of the Australian Province of the Dominicans. He has a doctorate in the history of 17th century philosophy from Deakin University. He recently published a history of the Sydney parish of Pyrmont (1867-2017), where he was parish priest from 2004 to 2013. *150 Years on Pyrmont Peninsula: The Catholic Community of Saint Bede 1867–2017*, is reviewed in this issue.

the country districts of the colony. One of the February 1838 arrivals, John Brady, was despatched to Penrith with the usual commission to build a church. Within months he would become the target of vicious sectarian journalism. A recent convert, Trinity College graduate, Charles Henry Chambers, would emerge as Brady's solicitor in the ensuing libel cases; in 1842 Chambers was appointed Sydney's first Town Clerk.

At the origins of this outburst of sectarianism was the mid-year arrival in the colony, not only of another batch of Irish clergy, but of a small book published in England by Ullathorne entitled *The Catholic Mission in Australasia*. The sixty page text had been produced in 1837 at Liverpool as a means of gaining the commitment of English and Irish bishops, priests and laity in supporting the Australian mission. It painted an alarming and pitiful picture of convict and emancipist life in the colony. Its impact on its intended audience was evident in the successful recruitment of priests and nuns. Its impact on the Sydney Tory establishment, the so-called 'Exclusives', was altogether negative. The *Gazette* announced the appearance of an 'eight-penny pamphlet' by the ultra-liberal Vicar General, 'the bosom friend of our late Governor Sir Richard Bourke', in which 'a most deplorable picture is given of the moral state of the Colony'.[2]

In a subsequent article the *Gazette* dedicated eleven columns to a mocking dismissal of the book's contents and its author. Six of the columns were taken up by direct quotes. Ullathorne was described as 'a dapper little gentleman of exceedingly mild and fascinating manners, more resembling in appearance what is generally called "a ladies' man" than a strict adherent of the stern doctrine of clerical celibacy'. The book was said 'to greatly resemble himself – having considerable more show than substance'. Ullathorne's purpose in condemning the transportation system was 'exposed': 'From the first page to the last, in every sentence, nay in every line, the one single aim and object – to work on the gullibility of simple John Bull, and finger his cash – is openly apparent.'[3]

The article highlighted and roundly rejected Ullathorne's description of convict conditions, drunken life in Sydney, the immorality of the native-born, the ineffectiveness of the Protestant clergy, the neglect of the aborigines. The criticism especially focused on those parts of the pamphlet which would put at risk the continuation of transportation. Debates about the future of the system were being held in the Westminster parliament and in the NSW Legislative Council. In April 1837 the British Parliament had established a Select Committee on Transportation chaired by the young radical parliamentarian, William Molesworth. On 8 and 12 February 1838

Ullathorne gave evidence to the committee to the effect that the system had failed altogether as a means of reformation of convicts, and that it led rather to their utter degradation. Following his appearance at the committee, Ullathorne published another pamphlet with the graphic title *The Horrors of Transportation Briefly Unfolded to the People*, a text that was yet to reach the colony.

Another Australian witness appearing at the Select Committee hearings in London was the Presbyterian minister, John Dunmore Lang, the eloquent opponent of the Exclusives. He mocked the Legislative Council, calling it 'our Colonial House of Lords'.[4] He gave strong representation to the Molesworth Committee about the evils of transportation and assignment labour. His Sydney newspaper, *The Colonist*, was forthright in its opposition to the continuation of the system:

> [W]e are decidedly of opinion, that the Transportation and Assignment System is in the present circumstances of this colony; utterly inefficient both as a system of penal discipline, and as a system of reformation, and that it ought therefore to be discontinued. This was the sum and substance of the evidence given by Dr. Lang, before the Transportation Committee in London.[5]

In its concluding report in August 1838 the Molesworth Committee recommended the 'immediate discontinuance of the practice of assigning convicts to settlers', the worst aspect of transportation, yet the one most profitable for the colonial establishment. Concerning transportation itself the committee recommended that it should be 'abolished and the penitentiary system of punishment be adopted in its stead as soon as practicable'.[6] Transportation to NSW ceased in 1840, but continued in other colonies and penal settlements until 1868. However, not even agreement on as important a policy as opposition to continued convict transportation could overcome primitive sectarian divisions in Sydney. The *Colonist* joined the Tory press in rejecting Ullathorne's pamphlet, castigating it as the 'sixpenny pamphlet ... which so outrageously *outherrods* Dr Lang'.[7]

It was in this tense atmosphere of politics and sectarianism that a journalist focused on newly arrived Father John Brady of Penrith. In August 1838 the *Gazette* carried an article about Brady seeking a donation towards the building of his church from a local Protestant landowner named Cox, many of whose assigned servants were Irish Catholics.[8] Brady had reason to expect a generous reception having already received offers of land for his church from two Protestant gentlemen of the district, Sir John Jamison and John Tindale. However, Cox refused to promote papist superstition and attacked his visitor's religion with a volley of texts from the Bible. There are three candidates for 'Squire Cox' – one or other of the brothers George, Henry and Edward, sons of William Cox the builder of the first road over the mountains to Bathurst, and the recipient of generous Government grants of land in the Penrith district. Each of the brothers had acquired properties at Mulgoa and built stately homes named Winbourne, Glenmore and Fernhill.

The journalist prefaced the story with assertions about the ignorance of Irish Catholic priests - 'many of these men have never read the Bible, and some of them had never handled it'. He then proceeded to identify Brady as one of these 'hedge-priests'. Brady had penned a letter to the squire expressing his surprise and disappointment at the reception he had received. It was this letter which was printed in the *Gazette,* and held up as 'quite equal in point of literary merit and originality of conception to any production of any *Hedge Priest'*. The article proceeded to make great fun of Brady's syntax, spelling and punctuation.[9]

A spirited defence was mounted by a Penrith parishioner who wrote a letter to the *Australian*, a newspaper at times more sympathetic to the Catholic community, explaining his pastor's poor written English by the fact that Irish was Brady's first language, and that he had spent the past nineteen years as a missionary on the Indian Ocean island of Bourbon, later named Réunion, speaking French. He cheekily concluded that if the scriptural debate were to be continued it would best be conducted in Hebrew or Greek, both languages known by Brady.[10] The *Gazette* simply fashioned more taunts from this explanation and continued the mockery of 'the Rev Father Jo Brady and his friends'.[11]

The attacks reached a climax on 18 September when the *Gazette* reprinted an article that had appeared in the *Colonist* a few days before. It was headed 'The Confessional'. Here was a classic anti-Catholic theme. Without naming Brady it told the story of a less than enthusiastic Catholic convert, 'an old wife' in the Penrith district, who held confessional practice in 'utter abhorrence':

> She got on tolerably well while there was no priest nearer than Parramatta or Windsor, because their visits to the district being only occasional, she was generally able to contrive some excuse for being out of the way, or shirking the duty. Latterly however a worthy priest has been stationed in the immediate neighbourhood, and such excuses being no longer of any use, go to confession she must.

Inevitably, as in every confessional story, the unnamed priest was accused of demanding money for his services, refusing 'to give her absolution unless she would immediately pay him down the sum of five pounds'. The story concluded: 'The indignant dame was compelled to comply, but she left the confessional protesting that be Catholics who may, she was determined in future to shelter herself under the wing of Bishop Broughton.'[12]

There was little doubt about who the unnamed 'worthy priest' was - the only priest stationed in Penrith was the Rev Father John Brady. The copied article was a continuation of the *Gazette*'s toying with 'Brady and Friends'. The harassment continued ten days after 'The Confessional' item in an article headed 'Father Jo Brady':

> Father Jo is most indubitably destined 'to live in story' - what with his abilities as an *illigant* letter-writer, his genuine *Hibernian* French idiom, and his very peculiar notions on the subject of the *presumptiousness* of 'laymen expatiating on the scriptures in the presence of a RC clergyman who has received a special mission *ad hoc*'. Father Jo evidently bids fair to throw Dr Ullathorne himself into the shade ... Father Jo has turned agitator, and has been trying his hand at the commendable occupation of attempting to upset convict discipline.[13]

There followed the saga, revealed the previous day in a letter to the *Sydney Herald*, of the refusal of a local landowner to allow his Catholic cook, an assigned convict, to attend Sunday Mass being conducted by Father Brady at the Penrith Police Office. The cook defied his master and attended Mass. The Master had him apprehended, but Brady intervened with the local police magistrate who arranged for a hearing the next day. The indulgent magistrate allowed the defendant to state his case, and in the words of the *Gazette*, 'Cookey set off and delivered himself of a rambling defence as intelligible as the explanations of the lower order of Irish usually are'. This was followed by Father Brady complaining that the landowner always prohibited his convict servants from attending Mass. The final outcome was that the unfortunate cook was sentenced to receive fifty lashes. The *Gazette* could not refrain from a final concluding flourish of mockery linking Brady's encounters with the two Penrith Protestant squires:

> Taught by sad experience the consequences of committing his ideas to paper, in a country where the French idiom is so very little understood as in Botany Bay, his Reverence resolved to try another plan, and attempted to bully Mr. Thompson into compliance by informing him that unless he did subscribe in aid of the erection of the Roman Catholic Chapel, his servants would not be allowed the benefit of clergy!!! That threat failing in its desired effect, Protestants not being

altogether so easily frightened at the bugbear of excommunication 'with bell, book, and candle' as would suit Father Jo's purposes, he seems to have fallen upon the plan of exciting insubordination among Mr. T's servants in order to bring him to reason.[14]

Unexpectedly on 13 October there was a change of tone with the appearance of an apology printed in the *Gazette*. It was occasioned by the editor's receipt of a letter on 8 October from 'a gentleman who acted on behalf of the Rev Mr Brady'. That gentleman was Brady's solicitor Charles Henry Chambers. The letter demanded the name of the author of the offending article and a copy of the manuscript which had reflected on the 'character and conduct of the Rev John Brady, who is clearly meant by "the priest stationed at Penrith".' This was unambiguously a letter preliminary to a libel action. The *Gazette*'s apology was published five days later:

> We think it but due to Mr Brady that we should at once retract the paragraph and apologise for having given it insertion. We do so the more readily because having bitterly had frequent occasion to come into contact with the same Rev gentleman, and having more than once handled his Reverence rather roughly, we would not willingly have it supposed that we would utter a syllable derogatory to his character except on the best possible authority. We shall be happy at all times to make the *amende honorable* whenever we find that we have inflicted a wound in error, or unintentionally.[15]

The apology was not accepted, and the cases for libel against the editors of *Colonist* and *Gazette* were finally heard in the Supreme Court in July 1839. The case against the editor of the *Colonist*, James McEachern, a Scottish school teacher who had been brought to the colony by Lang, the owner of the *Colonist*, came to court before Justice Alfred Stephen and a special jury on 9 October. Barristers for the plaintiff were Richard Windeyer, William Foster and the Attorney General, John Hubert Plunkett, who explained that he was a late substitute for Roger Therry. For the defendant were William a'Beckett and Edward Broadhurst. Bishop Polding was called as a witness in order to explain to the court the implications for the character and career of a priest accused of asking money as a condition of confessional absolution. The Bishop concluded that if Brady had been guilty of what was imputed of him in the newspaper article he would have been 'degraded to the last degree'.

The defence applied unsuccessfully for *nonsuit* or dismissal of the case on the grounds that 'the plaintiff had no *locus standi* as a Roman Catholic priest'. Judge Stephen ruled emphatically that:

The plaintiff, as a minister of religion, was as much entitled to damages as if he belonged to our own church; he was not to have the shield of justice removed from him because he differed from us in faith. While they remain subjects, all persons are entitled to the benefits of the laws, more especially a minister of the Christian faith - of a faith which, like our own, professes to be founded on Holy Writ.[16]

The principal defence was that the article was not a libel upon the individual, but a fair discussion on a public question, namely whether the practice of the confessional was the subject of ridicule and contempt, as Protestants contended. After instructions from the bench, the jury retired for fifteen minutes and returned a verdict in favour of the plaintiff and awarded damages of fifty pounds. The judge awarded costs against the defendant. Two days later the libel case against George Cavenagh of the *Gazette* came to the same court, with the Chief Justice, the recently knighted Sir James Dowling,[17] presiding, with Plunkett and Windeyer for the plaintiff, and a'Beckett and Foster for the defendant. The claim for damages was five hundred pounds.

The plaintiff's barristers argued a stronger case against Cavenagh because he had not only reprinted the article, already found to be libellous, but had, in presenting the story, attested to its authenticity, thus giving it more credibility in the eyes of the public. Polding was again called and cross examined. The defence placed much emphasis on the printed apology and turned the focus on the plaintiff's attorney, C H Chambers. A series of letters exchanged between Chambers and Cavenagh's solicitors from October 1838 to February 1839 were produced with the intention of showing that, with the encouragement of his greedy attorney, the plaintiff's sole motivation in refusal of the apology and persevering with the case was to achieve monetary gain for himself and his solicitor. The Chief Justice's instructions to the jury left them with little option but to find for the plaintiff, but the jurors revealed their sympathy for the defendant by awarding damages of one farthing.[18] The court eventually awarded costs against the defendant.

Both the *Colonist* and the *Gazette* continued their attacks on Brady, and now included Chambers in their sights. The *Colonist* in a style worthy of John Dunmore Lang set the tone in an article entitled 'The Confessional and no mistake!' It began: 'Father Brady will not surely now attempt to deny that he stipulates, expects, and rigorously exacts money for confessions, if not from Popish devotees, at all events, from Protestant Editors, when he drags them into Court!' It concluded:

We have only to say, however, that both Mr McEachern and our contemporary of *The Gazette* have been made to confess their editorial sins, both voluntarily and coercively; but they have at the same time demonstrated, or rather Father Jo himself has, that his object was not only to compel them to confess their fault, but also to make them pay pretty smartly for it, before he should absolve them from its consequences.[19]

The *Gazette* offered yet another reason for the libel cases, claiming that 'Father Jo Brady's action against the *Gazette* and *Colonist* newspapers was evidently got up in view of gagging the Protestant newspaper press of the Colony'. Chambers was described as Brady's 'compatriot', and in a footnote it was stated that 'Mr C H Chambers recently formally abjured the Protestant faith and turned Roman Catholic'.[20]

The final act in the long saga was the overnight imprisonment of McEachern for failing to pay damages and costs. This brought forth a parting outburst against Catholics, 'our ancient foes', and their 'malignant agent', Charles Henry Chambers:

And how has our forbearance been rewarded by our ancient foes and their zealous, but malignant agents? Let our infamous and never-to-be-forgotten incarceration tell how ... Has he [Chambers] exculpated himself from the charge of ungentlemanly precipitancy and want of courtesy ... in resorting so unceremoniously to such inquisitorial measures, in order to gratify the malignant feelings either of himself or his Catholic constituents, by subjecting us to personal contumely and degradation? No!!! and until he does so, we 'hold his honour light'.[21]

In a final blast entitled 'A Parting Salute' the *Gazette* on 8 October 1839 wrote:

Mr Chambers has got his costs, but we question whether he would not now gladly give five times the amount could he but sink the whole affair in oblivion; he has got his 'pound of flesh', but he has lost caste in public estimation, and he will find it difficult to regain it. Father Jo, too, has got his verdict - but, alas it is only a farthing! - Avarice and revenge both sought for gratification, and both have been disappointed ... We have now done with Mr CHARLES HENRY CHAMBERS. In the attempt to victimize us, he has himself become the victim.[22]

It was this one-sided power of press proprietors and editors to address, influence and persuade the public, and particularly in the onslaughts against Ullathorne and Brady, that led Bishop Polding to establish a Catholic newspaper which emerged in August 1839 as the *Australasian*

*Chronicle.* The proprietors were eight Irish emancipists. The Scottish convert, William Alexander Duncan, 28 years old, recruited by Ullathorne in England in 1838 for school teaching, and only nine months in the Colony, was appointed editor. Duncan, originally an aspirant to the Presbyterian ministry, was first attracted to Catholicism because of his disgust at newspaper onslaughts against the Church in Scotland, reasoning that such venom must point to something of great value.[23] In the first edition of the twice-weekly *Chronicle*, Friday 2 August, a 'prospectus' carried on the front page forcefully set out the purpose of the new publication:

> It has long been a matter of deep regret among a great and respectable portion of the inhabitants of this Colony, that, notwithstanding the great number of Newspapers published in Sydney, by far the greater part are strongly fettered by party influence, while not one has appeared, expressive of the wishes, or devoted to the interests of the Catholic Population. Placed, by the laws, on a perfect equality with other denominations of Christians, forming a third of the entire population, and inferior to none in the exercise of all the duties of good citizens, we are treated by a certain party as if we were a degraded caste - a cipher in the population; and we almost seem, as if we still groaned under the rigour of the penal laws. The Pulpit and the Press appear to vie with each other in promulgating the calumnies of the three last centuries, in misrepresenting our principles and abusing our laborious, respected, and highly exemplary Clergy. And, if, occasionally, a pen has been taken up in our defence, it has been to demand for us, not justice but toleration. To those who have vindicated us, though it has been, sometimes, at the expense of much that we respect, we are not ungrateful, but we feel that we ought to take higher ground. We must take our cause into our own hands. We must explain and defend our principles - wipe off the aspersions that have been cast upon us, and prove to our separated brethren, that we are worthy to join with them, hand in hand, in promoting the public good. To explain and uphold the civil and religious principles of Catholics, and to maintain their rights, will, then, be the primary objects of *The Australasian Chronicle*.[24]

In December Ullathorne boasted that the Church's victory over its press enemies in the Brady case had been a boon for the establishment of its own newspaper: 'The press which treated the Church with such unheard of violence is ruined ... The *Sydney Gazette*, the oldest paper in the Colony, backed by members of the [Legislative] Council and commercial influence – its Editor off to Port Phillip, and its materials, this day, put up for auction, and the best of these will be bought in by our party.'²⁵ In his autobiographical memoir, Duncan reminisced about the immediate impact of the *Chronicle*:

> At the time the Chronicle was established, the press of Sydney teemed with the most scurrilous, lying and obscene attacks upon everything connected with Catholicism. It was my primary duty to grapple with this mass of calumny, which I did in a manner that obtained for me not only torrents of applause from the catholic colonists, but the esteem and respect of many protestants; and I had soon the satisfaction of putting an end to this system of abuse, and of contributing to give a better tone to the colonial press than it had hitherto adopted.²⁶

The *Chronicle* was available for the defence of Brady when the original *Gazette* article of August 1838 was repeated verbatim in the controversial book published by Judge William Westbrooke Burton, *The State of Religion and Education in New South Wales*.²⁷ The author had cited the story as an example of how Catholic clergy unscrupulously sought money to build their churches. Brady's 'unlettered' missive was lifted out of ephemeral newsprint and given permanency between the hard-covers of Burton's book. In response Ullathorne wrote a scathing pamphlet which was serialised in the *Australasian Chronicle*. He directly addressed the 'Hedge Priest' slur:

> Mr. Burton introduces Fr Brady's letter into his book as a specimen of the education of a Catholic priest. Now, Mr Brady states in that letter that he was educated in France ... thence he passed to the Isle of Bourbon, where fifteen years of his life were spent in the ministry, daring which period he had not more than three or four opportunities of conversing in the almost forgotten tongue of his native country. When I first met the Rev Mr Brady in London, some two years previous to the date of that letter, he was from these circumstances unable to converse in English, and we were obliged to have recourse to the French language ... Let us suppose that Mr Burton's appointment had been to the Mauritius instead of to New South Wales. Let the first letter he should write in French after arrival, and address privately on private matters, be jeeringly thrown before the public through the channel of a newspaper, and be thence caught up by a grave dignitary and inserted in a work intended for permanency. Does this circumstance appear to Mr Burton as 'ludicrous', or as simply indecent?²⁸

Brady himself entered the lists again and wrote to the *Chronicle* asking that it publish his letter to the judge, written in French, accusing him of having 'borne false witness against. your neighbour'.²⁹ The reverend editor of the

*Australian* described the letter as 'libellous, calumnious, officious, insolent and ungentlemanlike'.[30] The feisty Duncan vigorously defended Brady, and so things continued.

One of the advantages of a Catholic press was the ability to print official church documents, such as the bishop's Pastoral Letters and pamphlets, which often contained more expansive responses to anti-Catholic publications. For example, for a shilling one could purchase 'A Reply to the Rev W Macintyre's *Candid Inquiry into the Doctrine maintained by Bishop Polding in his Pastoral Address*, by E. Hawksley', as advertised in the *Chronicle* of 10 April 1841.

Early in 1843 Duncan's editorship came to an abrupt end with his dismissal by the Vicar-General, Francis Murphy. Murphy was in charge of the Diocese while Duncan's patrons Polding and Ullathorne were absent in Europe. The Vicar-General acted against Duncan in the few remaining weeks before Polding's anticipated arrival back in Sydney. He claimed the support of all the clergy in his actions. In his letter to the Irish proprietors of the *Chronicle* explaining his decision he reiterated the reasons for establishing the newspaper:

> We wish to stand well with persons of every creed and honest public opinion—we are anxious to concede to others what we claim for ourselves, 'freedom of thought and action'; we wish well to all men of liberal and enlightened views—we desire not to be active partisans of any—we want no Dictatorship in politics or polemics, and we feel it high time to give public expression to these our sentiments, and to dissever ourselves in the eye of the public from the imprudent and injudicious conduct of Mr Duncan in this matter; we consider his zeal to have led him beyond that 'sobriety' of opinion so much recommended in holy writ, and that, instead of serving the cause he has undertaken to defend, he is seriously injuring the same.

He even implicated the absent Polding in the sacking: 'On the eve of the departure of our revered Prelate, he wrote a letter expressing his fears and anxiety regarding the incautious and over-zealous temper of Mr Duncan, and wishing him to be admonished on this head. The time has arrived when this admonition becomes a duty.'[31]

Duncan, with his chief patron Ullathorne absent and, in fact, never to return to the Colony, was vulnerable, but not crushed. Within days following his sacking he announced to the public, via a notice in the *Sydney Morning Herald*, that 'arrangements will shortly be made for the re-appearance of the true Chronicle'.[32] In March he wrote and had printed 'confidentially for private use', *An Appeal from the Unjust Decision of the Very Rev Vicar General Murphy to His Grace the Archbishop of Sydney*.[33] He argued in detail that his 'removal was effected by a scandalous combination of ecclesiastical influence and brute force, both alike contrary to honour, justice and equity'.[34]

Polding, on his arrival in Sydney as Archbishop and Metropolitan early in March, continued to be dependent on Duncan's adversarial skills; he commissioned him to produce a pamphlet in response to Bishop Broughton's attack on the pretensions and illegality of Polding's new titles.[35] However, Duncan soon realised that, because of the Archbishop's 'weakness' and 'timidity', he would not be reinstated as editor of the *Chronicle*: 'It was but too apparent that what the Archbishop was well inclined to do he dared not do in my behalf.' He sadly concluded: 'I who had been for three years his bosom friend, ceased altogether to visit the archiepiscopal residence, though often indirectly solicited to resume the intimacy'.[36]

Within six months of his dismissal Duncan had established his own newspaper, the *Weekly Register of Politics, Facts, and General Literature*. In the first number of the new journal he was unrepentant, still displaying an 'incautious and over-zealous temper':

> After having undergone a political martyrdom and having had our fabled deeds recorded in apocryphal Chronicles we rise again like the phoenix - somewhat emaciated in form, it will be perceived, as becomes our altered position and the state of the times, but unaltered in spirit, and firm as ever in our determination to contribute of such good sense, moderate acquirements, and honesty of purpose, as God has imparted to us, to support the rights and advance 'the position and interests of the people of our adopted country'.[37]

The *Weekly Register* ceased publication in January 1845, and Duncan relocated to Moreton Bay.

In May 1883, the *Freeman's Journal*, from 1850 the successor to the *Australasian Chronicle* as Sydney's Catholic newspaper, published a letter from 'Cassius' addressed to the aged William Augustine Duncan CMS, with high praise for his youthful contribution to journalism in Australia: 'From '39 to '42, your conduct of the AUSTRALASIAN CHRONICLE on Liberal Catholic lines made that journal a real power in the land.' 'Cassius' concluded:

> Disinterested, devoted, largely tolerant, affectionately loyal to your kind, watchful for their best and most vital interests, you bore the heat and burden of the day of crisis, with what a royal serenity of

mind, with what a high capacity for useful telling work, I sincerely trust the coming historian of this land will record with simple literal truth, nothing extenuating. Dowered with the hate of hate and scorn of scorn, in the fulness of your strength you wrought for and fought for the Just and the Right: hence it is that, though the grand results of your toil are not so generally credited to you as they should be, and will be, your old age is accompanied (as such an honoured age ought to be) with honour, love, obedience, troops of friends.[38]

Duncan died at his Sydney home on 25 June 1885.

**Notes**
1. *Sydney Gazette*, 17 July 1838.
2. *Sydney Gazette*, 7 July 1838.
3. *Sydney Gazette*, 12 July 1838.
4. *Colonist*, 11 July 1838.
5. *Colonist*, 11 July 1838.
6. Sir William Molesworth, *Speech on transportation delivered in the House of Commons on the 5th May 1840*, London 1840, p 76.
7. *Colonist*, 11 July 1838.
8. *Sydney Gazette*, 28 August 1838.
9. *Sydney Gazette*, 28 August 1838.
10. *Australian*, 31 August 1838.
11. *Sydney Gazette*, 1 & 11 September 1838. The repeated use the taunting phrase 'Father Jo' arose from the way in which Brady had signed his letter to Cox; he had simply used 'Jo' as an abbreviated form of 'John'.
12. *Sydney Gazette*, 18 September 1838.
13. *Sydney Gazette*, 27 September 1838.
14. *Sydney Gazette*, 27 September 1838.
15. *Sydney Gazette*, 13 October 1838.
16. *Sydney Herald*, 10 July 1839.
17. Sir James commented on his new title: 'The nickname has made many people wondrous civil to me' (C H Currey, 'Dowling, Sir James [1787–1844]', *Australian Dictionary of Biography*, National Centre of Biography, Australian National University, http://adb.anu.edu.au/biography/dowling-sir-james-1989/text2421, published in hardcopy 1966, accessed online 16 August 2016).
18. *Sydney Herald*, 12 July 1839
19. *Colonist*, 13 July 1839.
20. *Gazette*, 20 July 1839.
21. *Colonist*, 11 September 1839.

22 *Gazette*, 8 October 1839.
23 Margaret M Payten, *William Augustine Duncan, 1811-1885*: a biography of a colonial reformer, MA Thesis, University of New South Wales, 1965, p 10.
24 *Australasian Chronicle*, 2 August 1839.
25 Ullathorne to Brown, 4 December 1839. Quoted in Paul Collins, *William Bernard Ullathorne and the Foundation of Australian Catholicism 1815-1840*, Thesis submitted for the degree of Doctor of Philosophy of the Australian National University, 1989, 232.
26 W A Duncan, '*Autobiographical memoir*', 1854, manuscript in Mitchell Library, Sydney, NSW.
27 William Westbrooke Burton, *The State of Religion and Education in New South Wales*, London, 1840.
28 *Australasian Chronicle*, 3 October 1840.
29 *Australasian Chronicle*, 3 June 1841.
30 *Australian*, 8 June 1841.
31 *Australasian Chronicle*, 23 February 1843.
32 *Sydney Morning Herald*, 25 February 1843.
33 W A Duncan, *An Appeal from the Unjust Decision of the Very Rev Vicar General Murphy to His Grace the Archbishop of Sydney*, Sydney 1843.
34 Duncan, *An Appeal*, 13. See also J M O'Brien, 'W A Duncan, the Irish question and the NSW elections of 1843', *Journal of the Australian Catholic Historical Society*, 4 (1972), 40–57.
35 WA Duncan, *A letter to the Lord Bishop of Australia: containing remarks upon His Lordship's protest against the metropolitan and episcopal jurisdiction of His Grace the Archbishop of Sydney* (Sydney, 1843).
36 W A Duncan, '*Autobiographical memoir*', 54–55.
37 *Weekly Register*, 29 July 1843.
38 *Freeman's Journal*, 5 May 1883. It has been suggested that 'Cassius' was the pen name of J H B Curtis, formerly Father Anselm OSB (Payten, *William Augustine Duncan*, p iv, n 1). The more likely candidate was John Cash Neild, as clearly identified by the *Freeman's* 'Flaneur' in his responses to the many letters of 'Cassius' addressed, 'per favour of the *Freeman's Journal*', to Sydney notables from 1882 to 1884.

# Killing Conscription: the Easter Rising and Irish Catholic attitudes to the conscription debates in Australia, 1916-1917

## Jeff Kildea*

**Introduction**

During the First World War the Australian government twice asked the Australian people by plebiscite to approve the introduction of military conscription for overseas service. On each occasion, in October 1916 and December 1917, the Australian people by a narrow margin said no.[1]

After the defeat of the first referendum supporters of conscription casting around for a scapegoat to blame for their loss found one in the Irish Catholic community, which at the time made up about 22 per cent of Australian voters. Even the prime minister, William Morris Hughes, agreed, claiming that 'the selfish vote, and shirker vote and the Irish vote were too much for us'.[2] In August 1917 Hughes told his British counterpart David Lloyd George, 'The [Catholic] Church is secretly against recruiting. Its influence killed conscription'[3]

But it was not only supporters of conscription who believed that it was Irish Catholics embittered by Britain's treatment of Ireland in the wake of the Easter rising who swung the vote. The *Catholic Press*, which had opposed conscription, declared soon after the vote, 'And when the referendum campaign was swinging the electors, now "Yes", now "No", one heard with insistent frequency the question, "How can I vote 'Yes' while Ireland is under martial law?"'.[4] Labor's Frank Anstey wrote, '[I]f there had been no Easter Week in Ireland ... there would have been no hope of defeating conscription in Australia'.[5]

As we prepare to mark the centenary of the first conscription referendum next Friday week it is a good time for us as members of the Australian Catholic Historical Society to reflect on Catholic attitudes to conscription and to examine whether it was the Catholic Church, as Hughes claimed, which killed conscription and whether the Easter Rising had influenced the result.

**Conscription referendum 1916**

When in August 1916 Prime Minister Hughes returned from a visit to London, having been persuaded by the Army Council of the necessity

---

* Dr Jeff Kildea, Adjunct Professor in Irish Studies at University of New South Wales, a paper given to the Australian Catholic Historical Society, Sydney, on 16 October 2016.

for increased Australian reinforcements, he was determined to introduce conscription for overseas service—despite the difficulty he knew he faced in gaining the support of his own Labor Party and of the labour movement generally.[6] Because anti-conscription Labor senators held the balance of power in the Senate Hughes did not have the numbers to pass the necessary legislation.

He therefore decided to take the issue to the people in a plebiscite, hoping thereby 'to coerce the hostile Senate if the vote turned out to be in favour of conscription'.[7] Pro-conscriptionists were disappointed believing Hughes should have tested the resolve of the anti-conscription senators by having a proclamation issued immediately on his return to Australia. They argued that the Australian people would have accepted it and the senators would have fallen into line.[8]

## Preliminary points

At the outset, two preliminary points should be made. Firstly, the vote on conscription was not a constitutional referendum. The parliament already had power under the Constitution to pass the necessary legislation. The impediment to its doing so was not constitutional but political. Hughes did not have the numbers in the Senate.

Today Australians tend to use the term 'plebiscite' to describe such a non-binding vote by the people on a particular issue, such as the proposed vote on same-sex marriage. This is to distinguish it from a constitutional referendum, which is binding and which has a specific requirement that not only must a majority of the voters support the proposal but so too must the voters in a majority of states – the so-called 'double majority'.

However, in 1916 the term 'plebiscite' was hardly ever used even though the conscription vote was non-binding. The legislation enabling the vote on conscription was the *Military Service Referendum Act* and the prime minister and other campaigners as well as the press almost always used the term 'referendum' to refer to that vote.[9] The only newspaper which did not do so was *Truth*, whose editor Samuel Albert Rosa criticised Prime Minister Hughes for using the word 'referendum', not because it was constitutionally inaccurate but because it was ungrammatical. According to Rosa a 'referendum' is the question being referred to the people while a 'plebiscite' is the mechanism for doing so. But, apart from Rosa's dissent, 'referendum' was the generally accepted term.

Accordingly, when discussing the vote on conscription in its historical context, it is quite proper to refer to it as they did then, namely as a 'referendum'.

The second point to note is that the principal issue was not whether Australia should have conscription. Under amendments to the *Defence Act* in 1909 supported by all parties, military training had been compulsory for men and boys since 1911. But under the Act it was limited to service within Australia. Hughes wanted the *Defence Act* amended so as to extend conscription to overseas service, but he believed, on good grounds, the Senate would vote it down.

Another option possibly available to Hughes was an order or regulation under the *War Precautions Act*. But, again he would be at the mercy of the Senate, which had the power to disallow such instruments.[10]

So, Hughes considered that his only course of action was to appeal above the heads of the senators to the people so as to put moral pressure on them. Whether the anti-conscription senators would have backed down as the prime minister hoped will never be known, for the vote went against conscription.

What we do know is that Hughes opted for a referendum and that during the lengthy campaign the issue divided the Australian people and split the governing Labor Party, with Hughes walking out of the caucus in November 1916 and joining forces with the conservative Liberal Party to form a 'win-the-war' party that later became known as the Nationalist Party.

## Catholics and the defeat of conscription

After the vote was lost Hughes became obsessed with the role he perceived Australian Catholics of Irish descent had played and were playing in opposing his government's 'win-the-war' policies and himself personally.

In April 1917 he told his confidant in London Keith Murdoch, father of Rupert, that 'the bulk of Irish people led by Archbishop Mannix … are attacking me with a venomous personal campaign'.[11] In August 1917 he told Lloyd George,'[T]he Irish question is at the bottom of all our difficulties in Australia. They—the Irish—have captured the political machinery of the Labor organisations—assisted by syndicalists and I.W.W. people'.[12]

The IWW were the Industrial Workers of the World, a revolutionary working class movement that originated in the United States in 1905 and came to Australia in 1907. They were syndicalists, a term which denotes the use by the working class of industrial rather than political action to overthrow capitalism. The IWW rose to prominence in Australia during

World War I when its members were accused of acts of sabotage, including arson, aimed at subverting the war effort.[13]

Even before the vote was taken Hughes had been mindful of the impact events in Ireland might have on Irish Catholic voters, a consideration advanced in some of the Catholic newspapers. For example, the editor of Adelaide's *Southern Cross* wrote two weeks before the vote:

> No doubt the majority of Australian Catholics are opposed to conscription, but the reason will be found not in their Catholic principles, but in the fact that they are mainly Irishmen or descendants of Irishmen. Recent unhappy events in Ireland have revived the feeling against the British misrule of past centuries which it was hoped that the legislation of the last 25 years and the concession of Home Rule would obliterate.[14]

Hughes therefore sent a private message to the editor of the *Catholic Press*, one of Sydney's two Catholic newspapers, saying he would use his influence with the British government to have the Home Rule Act put into operation at once, if the *Catholic Press* ceased its opposition to conscription.[15]

New South Wales premier W A Holman, another supporter of conscription, instructed the state's agent-general in London to tell the British government that it would assist the 'Yes' vote if it were to end martial law in Ireland and commit itself to home rule. The New South Wales government also tried to convince Irish nationalist leader John Redmond to send a message to Australia supporting conscription. Redmond refused saying that he and his colleagues were busy opposing it for Ireland.[16]

A fortnight before the vote was taken Hughes told the commander of the Australian Imperial Force, Lieutenant General William Birdwood:

> The overwhelming majority of the Irish votes in Australia which represents nearly 25 per cent of the total votes has been swung over by the Sinn Feiners and are going to vote No in order to strike a severe blow at Great Britain.[17]

Protestant pro-conscriptionists shared Hughes' concern. The anti-Catholic pamphleteer Critchley Parker warned Protestant Australians before the 1916 referendum, 'It has to be remembered that Roman Catholics are voting for Ireland, not Australia, on Saturday'.[18] So too the Grand Master and the Grand Secretary of the Loyal Orange Institution of Queensland who warned their members and 'Protestants generally':

> [A] large proportion of the Roman Catholics within the Empire (and more especially within the Irish section of that Church), are holding

back from participating in the War, and the extremists amongst them are doing all in their power to prevent the War being carried to a successful termination. ... The venomous anti-English hate which has been for generations instilled into the Irish Catholic by his priesthood is bearing its fruit.[19]

After the vote was taken criticism of the Irish Catholic community intensified. In explaining to its readers why 'Contrary to all forecasts of sanity and patriotism regarding the referendum, the friends of the Kaiser have won', the *Australian Christian Commonwealth*, a Methodist weekly published in Adelaide, observed:

Strong support throughout the Commonwealth came to the 'No' army from the Roman Catholics. ... It is common rumour that their priests, with few exceptions, were openly or secretly opposed to conscription.[20]

And it was not only militant Protestant newspapers which ran that line. Melbourne's metropolitan weekly the *Leader* opined:

In Australia ... we are ... entitled to doubt whether Irish sympathy can be counted on in the vigorous prosecution of the war. ... Their attitude is dictated by racial animosities and political differences which a wiser judgment would have put aside under the critical conditions in which the whole nation is involved.[21]

These anti-Catholic and anti-Irish attitudes in the context of the war and the conscription referendum reflected views that were widespread in Australia even before the war and before the Easter rising. In 1913 the New South Wales member of parliament Thomas Henley MLA told a 'Grand Protestant Demonstration' in Sydney, 'The disloyalists of Australia are mostly Irish-Roman Catholics'. He put it down to the Catholic schools, which he described as 'seed-plots of disloyalty' where they taught the children 'to be disloyal to the Empire and to the Union Jack—the great Flag under whose protection they were growing up!' [22]

So, were Hughes and his supporters right when they claimed that the Irish Catholic community in Australia was involved in a sinister plot to undermine the war effort and to kill conscription?

## The Irish question, Australia and the War

To answer this question we need to look at the context in which the claims were made. In the early 20th century there was a strong correlation between religious affiliation and the three main national or ethnic groups that constituted European society in Australia: the English, the Irish and the

Scots. Competition between these groups reflected not only theological differences but also complex ethnic rivalries, particularly those between Irish Catholics on the one hand, and English Anglicans and Scots-Irish Presbyterians on the other. These rivalries, pre-dating European settlement in Australia but reinforced by local events, became endemic in the Australian political system during the 19th and early 20th centuries, intensifying in the years immediately before the war.[23]

When in 1912 the British government announced its intention to legislate for Irish home rule, a major controversy emerged in Australia between supporters and opponents of the proposal, who divided generally along ethno-religious lines. And it was not long before debate about the United Kingdom's constitution became entwined with local issues, particularly the demand by Catholics for state aid for their schools.

These sectarian tensions, which increased as the home rule debate dragged on, subsided after the outbreak of the war in August 1914. Partly this was due to the shelving of the issue in the United Kingdom—when the Home Rule Bill was enacted in September 1914 but suspended for the duration of the war—but also because Protestants and Catholics in Australia were prepared to set aside their differences to support the war effort.

For example, on 6 August 1914 the *Freeman's Journal*, one of Sydney's Catholic weeklies, opined:

> Few facts are susceptible of clearer demonstration than that vital issues as to the future of this country are at stake. Should England be beaten in a duel with Germany, Australia, too, would have her turn. Colonies is one of the Kaiser's dreams. Where could that dream be better realised than in this country? Adieu, then to that Australian independence of which we are all proud.[24]

However, in reality, the display of denominational unity was a fragile façade. Although the Catholic Church joined with the Protestant churches in supporting Australia's participation in the war, its commitment, unlike theirs, was not based on theological and imperial considerations. Most Protestant spokesman characterised the conflict as a righteous war against godless Prussianism, which they regarded as 'a threatening form of state religion ... inspired by a unique sense of mission to impose its hegemony by force over the world'.[25]

Australian Catholics, on the other hand, had a pragmatic, even utilitarian, view of the international conflict, regarding the war in terms of Australian interests. If Britain lost the war Australia would be at the mercy of German expansion in the western Pacific, where they already occupied a number of islands including a large part of New Guinea. Catholics also hoped that by sharing in the blood sacrifice they might enjoy increased tolerance and the satisfaction of their grievances, especially state aid for their schools.[26]

On 9 August 1914 Michael Kelly, the Catholic Archbishop of Sydney, told his congregation, 'We must forget all personal considerations and stand together as a nation. In Australia our little differences must be set aside, and as fellow-citizens we must stand shoulder to shoulder.' However, his idea of setting aside differences had a distinctly Catholic flavour: 'If this war pleased God, the people of the various religions would have such esteem for one another that there would be no more disabilities put upon their schools, and the question would not be asked in connection with their public work whether a person was a Catholic or not.'[27]

For the next twenty months talk of Irish Catholic disloyalty subsided, at least in public, as Catholics and Protestants lined up together at the recruiting offices to enlist in the Australian Imperial Force and to help the British Empire defeat Germany.[28] But the fragile truce in the sectarian conflict was broken following the Easter rising in April 1916.

When news of the outbreak of violence in Dublin during Easter week began to reach Australia, many leading Catholics of Irish descent condemned the rising, seeing it as a threat to the promised implementation of home rule. Even Archbishop Mannix, who soon would become closely identified with Irish republicanism, initially described the rising as deplorable and its leaders as misguided. However, the mood changed when General Sir John Maxwell began using harsh measures to restore order in Ireland. Following the execution of the leaders of the rising, the deportation of thousands of others and the imposition of martial law, Australian Catholics of Irish descent became openly critical of British rule in Ireland, provoking a Protestant backlash.[29]

Sectarianism, which had lain dormant since the outbreak of the war, flared up and intensified as many Protestants regarded such criticism as disloyal to the British Crown, already under threat from without but now also from within. It was in this highly-charged atmosphere that the first conscription referendum was held.

## Catholics and Conscription

As we have seen, one of the reasons Hughes gave to Lloyd George for the referendum's defeat was the influence of the Catholic Church. But there was nothing in Church teaching that prohibited compulsory military service for defence at home or overseas, and during the referendum campaign the Vatican's representative in Australia, Archbishop Bonaventura Cerretti, issued a statement making it clear that conscription was not an issue of faith or morals upon which the Church could direct its members.[30] Not surprisingly, therefore, Catholics held differing personal opinions on the government's proposal, including individual bishops, of whom only two expressed their views publicly in 1916.

Archbishop Patrick Clune of Perth was reported in newspapers across Australia as saying, 'Whoever believes in the righteousness and justice of the war we are engaged in ought not to hesitate to vote for compulsory military service in Australia',[31] while Archbishop Daniel Mannix, coadjutor Archbishop of Melbourne, spoke against conscription at just two public functions. At the opening of the September Fair at the Albert Hall, Clifton Hill on 16 September 1916, he told his audience that 'conscription is a hateful thing, and it is almost certain to bring evil in its train' and that 'Australia has done her full share – I am inclined to say more than her fair share in this war'.[32] On 22 October in replying to an address presented to him in the parish hall at Preston he said that he stood by what he had previously said and that he intended to vote against conscription.[33]

At the time Mannix was little known outside Victoria; certainly he was not the national figure he would become during the second referendum campaign in 1917. Among the Catholic laity there were also differences of opinion that found their way into the press, while Catholic newspapers adopted divergent viewpoints.[34] This reflected the way in which the country itself was divided over the issue.

Catholics opposed to conscription put forward a mixture of moral, political and economic arguments: compulsion was wrong; Australia had done its share and would be defenceless if more soldiers were sent to Europe; conscription would bring economic disaster to Australia; it would destroy trade unionism and lead to militarism; Australia would have to rely on foreign labour.[35] Although Catholic newspapers had criticised Britain's handling of events in Ireland during 1916, those newspapers opposed to conscription generally did not argue their case on anti-imperialist grounds. The *Catholic Press* and Adelaide's *Southern Cross* did, however, draw on two aspects of the Irish crisis to bolster the anti-conscription case, arguing firstly that if the 60,000 or more British troops enforcing martial law in Ireland were removed to France there would be no need to conscript Australians, and secondly that Australia's adoption of conscription would encourage England to introduce conscription in Ireland.[36]

Although the Catholic Church's official silence was in stark contrast to the loud and almost monolithic support of conscription by leaders of the Protestant churches,[37] Hughes' claim that the Catholic Church was secretly against recruiting and that its influence killed conscription cannot be sustained. In fact, shortly after the 1916 campaign, he acknowledged as much when he wrote to Conservative Party leader Andrew Bonar Law, 'What an unholy alliance this is between men who have no religion [the IWW], who openly scoff at anything that savours of religion and the great Catholic Church. Of course it is not the Church AS SUCH but the Irish who see in England's peril Ireland's opportunity'.[38]

**Conscription and Irish Catholic vote**

It soon became the orthodox view, among contemporaries and many historians, that the Irish Catholic vote was decisive and that the Easter rising and the British government's response to it was a major factor influencing Australian Catholics of Irish descent to oppose conscription. Even the *Catholic Press*, one of the few newspapers in New South Wales to oppose conscription but which hardly mentioned Ireland in its editorials on the issue, claimed Britain's treatment of Ireland had been decisive, declaring immediately after the vote, 'It would be futile to deny that the continuance of martial law in Ireland was perhaps the strongest factor in swelling the 'no-conscription' returns'.[39]

On the fiftieth anniversary of the rising distinguished historian Ken Inglis wrote:

> In Australia [the rising] had pulled the cork out of the bottle of sectarian hatred at exactly the moment when WM Hughes resolved that men must be compelled to fight for the Empire. ... Had it not been for the Sinn Feiners and Sir John Maxwell, Australian conscripts would have gone to France.[40]

Subsequent research, however, has contradicted this view.[41] While historians generally accept that the majority of Catholics in Australia voted against conscription, the research suggests that they were influenced more by their working-class background and other local factors than by events in Ireland or their religious adherence.

Labour historian Ian Turner questioned the orthodoxy in his 1962 PhD thesis, where he argued:

> There is no general correlation between Catholicity and the 'No' vote: New South Wales and Victoria, both with a higher than average Catholic element in their populations, behaved oppositely, while the

biggest movement towards 'No' came in the South Australian country electorates, where the proportion of Catholics was well below the average.[42]

In a detailed article examining the Irish Catholic vote in the referenda, historian Alan Gilbert wrote in 1969:

> Most Irish-Catholics would have opposed conscription even if there had been no rising in Ireland during the War; some voted YES despite the Rising. Commitment to Labour politics, belief in the primacy of national over imperial interests, and concern about the possible conscription of Catholic teaching brothers were more important than Irish affairs in prompting many Catholics to vote NO.[43]

Nevertheless, he added:

> Irish affairs had a profound effect on the mood of Irish-Catholics in Australia, and secured for anti-conscription some of that fairly small minority of Irish-Catholic votes which would otherwise have endorsed the Government's proposals.[44]

However, in Patrick O'Farrell's opinion, events in Ireland did not teach Australian Catholics anything they did not already know from their knowledge of Irish history and their own struggles over the previous fifty years. Rather, it served to remind them 'that the dominant forces in Australian society sought to exclude or demean Catholics of Irish origin.'[45] Naomi Turner, in her two-volume history of Australian Catholicism, concurred: 'Realistically, [Australian Catholics] looked at the Australian situation with its direct effects on them, rather than that of the Irish.'[46]

In the same vein, Mark Lyons in his 1966 BA Honours thesis wrote:

> Ireland did play a large part in the consciousness of many of her children overseas, but the reason for this lies more in the position which these children occupied within the new society overseas, and it was that reality which was much more significant in forming their response to events within the new country.[47]

In another undergraduate thesis in 1977, Virginia Murray argued:

> Undoubtedly, the Easter Uprising reinforced ideas of Irish nationalism, hardened anti-British sentiments, and was an important factor in insulating the majority of Catholics from Imperial patriotism. The treatment that Ireland was to receive from England would have influenced some to vote NO.
>
> But the problem extends beyond the Easter Uprising. For a greater understanding, attention must also be directed towards their sense

of Australian nationalism and the effect that the sectarian issue was to have upon them. Although these two factors were in some ways connected to the repercussions of the Easter Uprising, they were also important by themselves in moulding Catholic opinion.[48]

These qualitative opinions are supported by quantitative research.

In his 1971 PhD thesis, Terry Metherall, who later became education minister in the New South Wales government, undertook a detailed examination of the voting patterns in each of the electorates. As regards the Irish Catholic vote, he concluded:

> [I]f anything emerges clearly concerning the 'Roman Catholic vote' in the referenda it is that Catholics voted along lines of class and economic interest rather than religion. The Irish Catholic lot, in particular, was inextricably bound up with that of the Labor party because the Irish Catholics were almost all labourers, share croppers, small farmers and shopkeepers. As the attacks upon Archbishop Mannix by leading judges in Victoria and NSW suggested, when Catholics rose above the working class they adopted the values and prejudices of their higher station.[49]

In 1982 Glenn Withers confirmed Metherall's conclusion with a statistical analysis of voting returns for each electorate. Using multi-variate regression analysis Withers found:

> The results for [the] Catholic population, in particular, while consistently negative are relatively small in magnitude and not of great statistical significance. This is, of course, consistent with the views of those writers ... who stressed the Catholic vote may have been divided.[50]

According to Withers the only statistically significant factor operating in favour of the No vote was membership of organised labour.

On the other hand, Jenny Tilby Stock in her quantitative analysis of the rural vote in South Australia based on electoral subdivisions found that "Germans" and Irish Catholics who belonged to cohesive ethnic-religious communities were distinctly less enamoured of conscription than were those of "British" birth and descent', but she also found that the propensity to vote for or against conscription depended on:

> the nature of the primary production being conducted, with farmers engaged in vine growing, dairying, sheep and, to a lesser-extent, hay production being more likely to resist conscription than those growing wheat.[51]

She observed that it was for other researchers to establish the extent to which factors influencing the farming vote in South Australia applied to other states. So far such detailed statistical analysis at subdivisional level has not been carried out across the Commonwealth.

**'The Roman Catholic Menace'**

Whatever the reality, as revealed by this historical research, it was the perceived role of the Irish Catholic vote in the conscription referenda which was important. As Labor historian Denis Murphy wrote in 1974:

> Clearly there was no simple correlation between Catholicism, Protestantism and conscription, though it would be foolish not to accept that the Easter rebellion had some effect on how a large number of Catholics voted. What was important for Australian politics was that conscriptionists accepted that there was a link between Irish Catholicism and the defeat of conscription.[52]

This perception was to become the occasion of some of the most vitriolic attacks ever made on the Irish Catholic community in Australia. Irish-Catholic assertiveness in public affairs was to provoke a Protestant backlash—the fury of which was magnified by the humiliation Hughes and his pro-conscription supporters had suffered as a result of the rejection of the government's proposals. Charges of disloyalty and plotting to overthrow the Empire added a more sinister dimension to the customary sectarian taunts.

Soon after the first referendum, the *Methodist* newspaper, in an article headed 'The Roman Catholic Menace' warned its readers of 'the personal predominance of Roman Catholics in the trades unions and the political labor leagues' and added:

> Roman Catholicism is subtly working ... to secure ascendancy and control. That church is working in the interests of disloyalty and of sectarian advantage, and is throwing dust in the eyes of Protestant electors all the time, especially of the working classes.[53]

Epithets such as 'Shirkers', 'Sinn Feiners', 'IWWers' and 'pro-German' became commonplace.

On 12 March 1917 Billy Hughes complained to Lloyd George through his London confidant Keith Murdoch:

> Australian recruiting is practically at a standstill. Irish National Executive here has carried resolution to effect that until Home Rule granted no Irish Catholics shall join forces. This is being acted on and

in such a way that the non-Irish population are going out of Australia to fight ... . The Irish remain behind and in any election their voting strength is greatly increased.[54]

This was nonsense. Recruiting was not at a stand-still in March 1917, averaging just over 6000 per month in the last three months of 1916 and over 4800 per month in the first three months of 1917, with the decline occurring across the whole population and not just among Irish Catholics. Throughout the war Catholics served in the AIF roughly in proportion to their numbers in the population, a fact which was known at the time and which has been confirmed since.[55]

Allegations began to circulate in otherwise responsible circles of an association between the Catholic Church and the IWW. Rev. W F Wentworth Shields, the Anglican Bishop-elect of Armidale, accused the Catholic body of being 'drawn together into an evil partnership with the IWW'.[56]

The growing anti-Catholic animus was stirred up even more in January 1917, after Archbishop Mannix described the war as 'an ordinary trade war', reported in some newspapers as 'a sordid trade war'.[57] This and other public utterances by Mannix, critical of the government's war policy, elevated him to national status and earned him the role of bogey man in the minds of the government's supporters and a hero to its opponents.

In May 1917 Mannix succeeded Archbishop Thomas Carr as the Archbishop of Melbourne, raising his profile even more. He soon assumed the mantle of leader of the opposition to Hughes' 'win-the-war' party, answering calls for a greater war effort in support of the Empire by pointing to Britain's betrayal of Ireland and arguing that the duty of Australians was to Australia first. He soon became the accepted spokesman of the Irish Catholic community in Australia, while at the same time he became a lightning-rod attracting much of the rising anti-Catholic and anti-Irish bigotry.[58]

Many of Australia's Irish Catholics, particularly those who had climbed the social ladder, were embarrassed by Mannix's outspokenness. Their embarrassment deepened when the archbishop exhorted Australian Catholics to adopt 'the Sinn Fein spirit'. At a rally in support of Irish independence held at Richmond racecourse on 6 November 1917 attended by over 100,000 people, Archbishop Mannix said:

> You in Australia are Sinn Feiners, and more luck to you. To you Australia is first and the Empire second.[59]

At one level it could be said that this meant no more than 'self reliance' expressed at the ballot box, however, to many Protestant Australians, particularly those already fearful of Roman domination, an evocation of 'the Sinn Fein spirit' was a call to violence and revolution, a call to emulate those who were opposed to Britain and the Empire.

One of the well-to-do Catholics embarrassed by Mannix's utterances was Dr Herbert Moran, who wrote in his memoirs:

> We Catholics became like a substance held in suspension but never quite in solution. ... Under the commotion of the Great War, in the first year of danger from without, our whole population assumed for a while the appearance of a clear and elegant mixture. It was an Archbishop's mischief which threw us down again, as a cloudy precipitate.[60]

But Mannix was not the only Irish Catholic to challenge the prime minister and his 'win-the-war' party. Queensland premier Thomas Joseph Ryan, the Catholic son of an illiterate Irish farm labourer and an Irish mother, emerged after the 1916 vote as another leader of anti-government opinion.[61] It was in his state that Hughes suffered the indignity of being struck by an egg thrown by an Irish Australian, Bart Brosnan.

The incident occurred at Warwick on 29 November 1917, three weeks before the second conscription referendum. To make matters worse, an Irish Australian policeman, Sergeant Henry Kenny, refused to arrest the egg-thrower, according to Hughes' account of the incident. As a result Hughes drew up a regulation to establish a Commonwealth police force. In a telegram to the Governor-General, he explained:

> This will apply to Queensland where present position is one of latent rebellion. Police is honeycombed with Sinn Feiners and I.W.W. ... [T]here are towns in North Queensland where the Law ... is openly ignored and I.W.W. and Sinn Féin run the show.[62]

Hughes' difficulty with Irish Australia seems to have struck a chord with Lloyd George, who on 1 January 1917 told the War Cabinet that Hughes would not be able to attend the proposed Imperial War Conference in London 'as the lack of settlement in Ireland was causing trouble in Australia'.[63] On 25 April 1917 he told Frances Stevenson, his personal secretary and mistress:

> At every stage...the Irish question is a stumbling-block in the conduct of the war. It ought to have been settled last year. ... It has done much harm in Australia. Hughes begged me last year to settle it for the sake of Australia, but I failed to do so. Twice since then he has sent me messages saying that it is essential that the matter be settled.[64]

In his criticism of the Irish, Hughes demonstrated a fundamental lack of appreciation of the attitude of Irish Australians to the Irish question. While radical organisations such as the Irish National Association shared Sinn Féin's desire for an independent Irish republic, they represented a minority of Irish Australian opinion, which overwhelmingly supported home rule. Despite this, Hughes was prepared to brand Australian home-rulers as Sinn Féiners, even though he himself favoured home rule and the Australian parliament passed resolutions supporting it in March 1917.[65]

Although Hughes made representations to the British government to end martial law in Ireland and to implement home rule, 'the image which Hughes projected publicly was of the abrasive anti-Sinn Féiner, constantly harassed by his disloyal Irish republicans, intent ... on "control of the Commonwealth government"'.[66] This was an image Hughes was happy to promote, given the fact that more than 75 per cent of the electorate was Protestant and ill-disposed toward Sinn Féin's agitation for Irish independence at a time when Britain and the Empire were fighting for their survival.

**Conclusion**

Accepting that a majority of Australia's Irish Catholics voted against conscription, their numbers were too small to kill conscription as Hughes claimed. To single out Irish Catholics is to deny the significant role played by the largely Protestant working-class movement in mobilising the anti-conscription vote. Catholic anti-conscriptionists did play a significant part in the campaign, but their contribution to the outcome—particularly that of Archbishop Mannix—has been exaggerated, both by commentators at the time and by many historians thereafter.[67]

For some Catholics of Irish descent Britain's treatment of Ireland may have been a reason to vote against conscription, but, if so, it was but one among many reasons to vote that way and in all likelihood a product of the same factors which led them to oppose conscription in the first place.

The myth of a monolithic Catholic community led by Archbishop Mannix being the cause of the defeat of conscription gained currency, because it suited both sides. It enabled Hughes and anti-Catholic bigots to blame the 'disloyal' Irish Catholics for their failure to persuade a majority of their compatriots to vote in favour of conscription. And it suited Catholic activists, anxious to unify Catholic support behind efforts to advance Catholic interests, such as state aid for Catholic schools, to be able claim there was solidarity among Catholics which translated into a 'Catholic vote'.[68]

But, contrary to the claims of sectarian warriors, opposition to conscription did not necessarily equate with opposition to the war or the British Empire. The Irish Catholic community in Australia, on the whole, supported the war effort, enlisting in proportion to their numbers in the population. Even though their rate of enlistment declined in 1917 and 1918, it did so in line with that of the general population; not because of events in Ireland but rather because of declining enthusiasm for a war that had gone on too long and had claimed too many Australian lives.

**Notes**
1. In 1916 the 'No' majority was 72 476 out of a total of 2 247 590 formal votes. Three states recorded 'Yes' majorities (Victoria, Western Australia and Tasmania) and three 'No' (New South Wales, Queensland and South Australia). In 1917 the 'No' majority was 166 588 out of a total of 2 196 906 votes cast. This time Victoria joined the 'No' majority while Tasmania's 'Yes' majority was only 379 out of a total of 77 383 votes cast (Ernest Scott, *Australia during the war*, Angus & Robertson, Sydney, vol. XI of *The official history of Australia in the war of 1914–18*, 1936, p. 352, 427).
2. Letter 6 November 1916 to Andrew Bonar Law quoted in LF Fitzhardinge, *The Little Digger 1914-1952*, Angus & Robertson, Sydney, 1979, p. 215.
3. Letter quoted in Fitzhardinge, *The Little Digger*, p. 276.
4. *Catholic Press* 2 November 1916, p. 26.
5. Letter (undated) to Harry [Maddison?] quoted in Fitzhardinge, *The Little Digger*, p. 217.
6. Fitzhardinge, *The Little Digger*, pp. 171–172; Ian Turner, *Industrial Labour and Politics: The Dynamic's of the Labour Movement in Eastern Australia 1900-1921*, Hale & Iremonger, Sydney, 1979, pp. 98–104.
7. HV Evatt, 'Australia on the home front 1914–1918', *Australian Quarterly*, vol. 9, 1937, pp. 69–75 at 69–70.
8. See, for example, statements of Sir William Irvine, Senator Edward Millen and Tasmanian premier JH Lee (*Argus* 31 August 1916, p. 6).
9. A search of Trove on 19 July 2016 using the search phrase 'conscription AND plebiscite' yielded 115 hits: 44 from the decade 1910-1919; 7 from 1930-1939; and 64 from 1940-1949. Of the 44 from 1910-1919, 17 were from 1916, 26 from 1917 and 1 from 1918. This is to be contrasted with the results of a search using the phrase 'conscription AND referendum', which yields 11,155 hits: 10,137 from 1910-1919 of which 3652 were for 1916, 4671 for 1917, 1437 for 1918 and 371 for 1919.
10. Ernest Scott, *Australia during the War*, p. 361 states that Hughes could count on 11 supporters among the 31 Labor senators and the 5 Liberal senators giving him a total of 16 out of 36 votes in the Senate.
11. From a cable sent in April 1917, quoted in Fitzhardinge, *The Little Digger*, p. 286.
12. Quoted in Fitzhardinge, *The Little Digger*, p. 276.
13. See Verity Burgmann, *Revolutionary industrial unionism: the Industrial Workers of the World in Australia*, Cambridge University Press, Cambridge, 1995, pp. 192–202; Frank Cain, *The Wobblies at war: a history of the IWW and the Great War in*

*Australia*, Spectrum, Melbourne, 1993; Ian Turner, *Sydney's burning*, Alpha Books, Sydney, 1969.
14 *Southern Cross* 13 October 1916, p. 10.
15 PS Cleary, *Australia's Debt to Irish Nation-Builders*, Angus & Robertson, Sydney, 1933, p. 250.
16 L L Robson, *The First AIF: A Study of its Recruitment 1914-1918*, Melbourne University Press, Carlton, 1982, pp. 91-93.
17 Cable 14 October 1916, Hughes to Birdwood, quoted from *Smith's Weekly* 24 October 1936 in HV Evatt, *Australian Labour Leader: the Story of WA Holman and the Labour Movement*, Angus & Robertson, Sydney, 2nd edn, 1942, p. 415.
18 Critchley Parker, *The Slippery Way, Patriotic Pamphlet No. 16*, Melbourne 1916, p. 14, quoted by Alan D Gilbert, 'The Conscription Referenda, 1916-1917: The Impact of the Irish Crisis', *Historical Studies*, Volume 14, 1969, pp. 54-72 at p. 54.
19 *Watchman* 26 October 1916, p. 5. The Watchman was an outspoken Protestant weekly published in Sydney that circulated nationally.
20 *Australian Christian Commonwealth* 3 Nov 1916, p. 3.
21 *Leader* 16 December 1916, p. 29. The Leader was a weekly newspaper published by Melbourne's daily broadsheet the Age.
22 *Watchman* 6 February 1913, pp. 1-2. Henley's 'seed-plots of disloyalty' was an allusion to the Catholic criticism of state-run schools as 'seed-plots of future immorality, infidelity, and lawlessness' contained in a Joint Pastoral Letter issued by the Catholic bishops in 1879.
23 For a discussion of the meaning of 'sectarianism' in the Australian context see Jeff Kildea, *Tearing the Fabric: Sectarianism in Australia 1910–1925*, Citadel Books, Sydney, 2002; Michael Hogan, *The Sectarian Strand: Religion in Australian History*, Penguin Books, Ringwood, 1987, pp. 4–8; Mark Lyons, 'Aspects of Sectarianism in New South Wales circa 1865 to 1880', Ph.D. thesis, Australian National University, 1972, pp. viii–xxi.
24 *Freeman's Journal* 6 August 1914, page 22.
25 John A Moses, 'Australian Anglican leaders and the Great War, 1914–1918: the "Prussian Menace", conscription and national solidarity', *Journal of Religious History*, vol. 25 no. 3, October 2001, pp 306–323, 309; see also Robert D Linder, *The long tragedy: Australian evangelical Christians and the Great War, 1914–1918*, Openbook Publishers, Adelaide, 2000.
26 Kildea, *Tearing the fabric*, pp. 116–118. See also Michael McKernan, *The Australian churches at war: attitudes and activities of the major churches 1914–1918*, Catholic Theological Faculty, Manly, 1980, p. 30; Michael McKernan, *The Australian people and the Great War*, Nelson, Sydney, 1984, p. 19; Michael McKernan, 'Catholics, conscription and Archbishop Mannix', *Historical Studies*, vol. 17, 1976, pp. 299–314. Although Japan was on the Allied side in the war, fear of Japan had been an important element in the evolution of defence policy in Australia since Japan's victory over China in 1895 (Henry P Frei, *Japan's southward advance and Australia from the sixteenth century to World War II*, Melbourne University Press, Melbourne, 1991, p. 2). It was believed that Britain's defeat in the war would leave Australia exposed to the perceived imperial ambitions of Germany and Japan in the south-west Pacific.

27 *Freeman's Journal*, 13 August 1914, page 21.
28 The absence of public attacks on the Irish Catholic community in the first 20 months of the war may also have had something to do with the government's instructions to the censor on ways of 'minimizing harmful agitation and resentment among our people of Irish descent' (Fitzhardinge, *The Little Digger*, pp. 60–61).
29 *Advocate* 6 May 1916, p.25; *Freeman's Journal* 4 May 1916, p. 25; *Catholic Press*, 11 May 1916, p. 21; Kildea, *Tearing the fabric*, pp. 134–136; Peter Overlack, "Easter 1916' in Dublin and the Australian press: background and response', *Journal of Australian Studies*, no. 54/55, 1997, pp. 188–193; RP Davis, 'Tasmania and the Irish revolution, 1916–22', *Tasmanian Historical Research Association: Papers and Proceedings*, vol. 21 no. 2, 1974, pp. 69–88.
30 *Freeman's Journal* 5 October 1916, p. 23; *Catholic Press* 5 October 1916, p. 25
31 This was in a cable to the Defence Minister, Senator GF Pearce of Western Australia, which was reported in the newspapers, including those in the eastern states (Bobbie Oliver, *War and peace in Western Australia: the social and political impact of the Great War 1914–1926*, University of Western Australia Press, Nedlands, 1995, p. 117). The *Sydney Morning Herald* published the text of Archbishop Clune's cable twice (21 October 1916, p. 16; 27 October 1916, p. 6).
32 *Advocate* 23 September 1916, p. 25.
33 *Advocate* 28 October 1916, p. 23.
34 For a description of these divergent views see Kildea, *Tearing the fabric*, pp. 138–142.
35 Kildea, *Tearing the Fabric*, pp. 138-140.
36 *Catholic Press* 19 October 1916, p. 20; 26 October 1916, p. 20; *Southern Cross* 13 October 1916, p. 10.
37 It was not absolute, however. For example, a group of nine ministers from various Protestant denominations signed a 'Manifesto from Protestant ministers— 'Conscription and Christianity'—opposing conscription. A copy is in the Riley Collection in the La Trobe Library, Melbourne. For a description of some of the activities of Protestant pacifists and anti-conscriptionists see Bobbie Oliver, *Peacemongers: conscientious objectors to military service in Australia 1911–1945*, Fremantle Arts Centre Press, South Fremantle, 1997, pp. 40–43.
38 House of Lords Record Office, Bonar Law Papers BL/53/4/15, quoted in Jill Kitson, *Patriots Three: Billy Hughes, Lloyd George and Keith Murdoch during World War I*, ABC Books, Sydney, 2005, p. 75.
39 *Catholic Press* 2 November 1916, p. 26.
40 *Sydney Morning Herald* 9 April 1966, p. 11. Inglis was less dogmatic as to the influence of the Easter rising in 'Conscription in Peace and War, 1911-1945', *Journal of History Teachers' Association of NSW, October 1967*, pp. 5-41 at 21.
41 Peter Bastian, 'The 1916 conscription referendum in New South Wales,' *Teaching History*, vol. 5, 1971, pp. 25–36 and J Alcock, 'Reasons for the rejection of conscription—1916–1917,' *Agora*, vol. 7 (1973), pp. 185–194 survey some of the literature on the issue while Turner, *Industrial labour and politics*, pp. 113–116 canvasses a number of the hypotheses, concluding that it was the farmers, normally non-Labor, who were the decisive factor in the referendum's defeat. In 1976 Michael McKernan wrote, 'The Catholic response [to conscription] was a class response much

more than a religious or national one' ('Catholics, Conscription and Archbishop Mannix', *Historical Studies*, Vol 17, 1976, pp. 299-314 at p. 300).

42  Ian Turner, 'Industrial Labor and Politics: The Dynamic's of the Labour Movement in Eastern Australia 1900-1921', *ANU*, 1962, p. 202, published by ANU in 1965 and Hale & Iremonger in 1979.

43  Gilbert, 'Conscription Referenda', p. 54. On the proposal to conscript teaching brothers see Jeff Kildea, 'Australian Catholics and conscription in the Great War', *Journal of Religious History*, vol. 26, number 3, October 2002, pp. 298–313.

44  Gilbert, 'Conscription Referenda', p. 71.

45  Patrick O'Farrell, *The Irish in Australia*, New South Wales University Press, Kensington, 1993, pp. 270–273.

46  Naomi Turner, *Catholics in Australia: a social history*, Collins Dove, North Blackburn, 1992, vol. 1, p. 305.

47  M Lyons, 'Catholics and Conscription: A Study of Attitudes, N.S.W. 1916-1917', University of New South Wales, Arts IV Thesis, 1966, p. 14.

48  V I Murray, 'Archbishops, Editors and Conscription: A Study of the Catholic Church in Victoria and New South Wales, 1916-1917', Monash University, BA (Hons) Thesis, 1977.

49  T A Metherall, 'The Conscription Referenda, October 1916 and December 1917: An Inward-Turned Nation at War', PhD thesis, University of Sydney, 1971, p. 277.

50  Withers,'The 1916–1917 Conscription Referenda: A Cliometric Re-appraisal', *Historical Studies*, Vol 20, 1982, pp. 36-46 at p. 43. Murray Goot, an academic analyst of public opinion, has recently argued that Withers' modelling is invalid as it suffers from 'ecological fallacy', using 'data about *groups* as if they were data about *individuals*'. He says this is a common problem with most explanations of the referendum results and suggests that the 'close study of voting returns within subdivisions combined with other evidence of a quantitative or qualitative kind' should be pursued in the future (Murray Goot, 'The results of the 1916 and 1917 conscription referendums re-examined' in Robin Archer et al, *The Conscription Conflict and the Great War*, Monash University Press, Clayton, 2016, pp. 123-125, 145).

51  Jenny Tilby Stock, 'Farmers and the rural vote in South Australia in World War I: The 1916 conscription referendum', *Historical Studies*, Vol 21 No 84, 1985, pp. 391-411.

52  D J Murphy, 'Religion, Race and Conscription in World War I', *Australian Journal of Politics and History*, Volume 30, 1974, pp. 155-163 at p. 161. [Emphasis added]

53  *The Methodist*, 25 November 1916, p. 25.

54  Quoted in Fitzhardinge, *The Little Digger*, p. 261.

55  L L Robson 'The origin and character of the First AIF, 1914–18: some statistical evidence', *Historical Studies*, vol. 15, no. 61, 1973, pp. 737–48 at pp. 740–41, 748. See also Jeff Kildea, *Anzacs and Ireland*, UNSW Press, Sydney, 2007, ch. 3. In June 1917, the Defence Department released figures which showed that 18.57 per cent of those embarking for overseas service were Roman Catholics. According to the 1911 Census 20.14 per cent of the male population had given Roman Catholic as their religion (*Catholic Press* 28 June 1917, p. 26-27; cf. *Argus* 23 June 1917, p. 18).

56  *Catholic Press* 23 November 1916, p. 19.

57 Reports of Mannix's speech appearing the next day in the *Age*, and during the week in the *Advocate* and the *Tribune* used the word 'ordinary'. However, in an early edition of the *Argus* the expression 'a sordid trade war' appeared. In later editions, however, the word 'sordid' is illegible as if the printing plate has been mutilated. In the 3 February 1917 edition of the *Australasian*, a weekly newspaper published by the *Argus*, the word 'sordid' has been omitted altogether (Cyril Bryan, *Archbishop Mannix: champion of democracy*, The Advocate Press, Melbourne, 1918, pp. 72; photographic copies of the articles are reproduced at pp. 232–235; See also James Franklin, G O Nolan and M Gilchrist, *The Real Archbishop Mannix: From the sources*, Connor Court, Ballarat, 2015, pp. 13-14. Even the Governor-General in a despatch to London reported that Mannix had said 'sordid trade war' (Robson, *The First AIF*, p. 148).
58 Fitzhardinge, *The Little Digger*, p. 286.
59 *Freeman's Journal*, 8 November 1917, page 27; Franklin, Nolan and Gilchrist, *The Real Archbishop Mannix*, pp. 28-33.
60 Herbert Moran, *Viewless Winds: Being the Recollections and Digressions of Australian Surgeon*, Peter Davies, London, 1939, p. 22.
61 D J Murphy, *T J Ryan: a political biography*, University of Queensland Press, St Lucia, 1975, p. 11.
62 Fitzhardinge, pp. 291–295. It was quite a mêlée and, as might be expected, accounts are confused. Even Fitzhardinge seems to be unclear as to whether Brosnan was arrested or not and whether it was Bart or his brother Pat who threw the egg that hit Hughes.
63 Fitzhardinge, *The Little Digger*, p. 252.
64 Quoted in *Patriots Three*, p. 82, cited as HLRO [House of Lords Record Office] Lloyd George Papers FLS/4/4.
65 John O'Brien, 'The Irish revolutionary movement and WM Hughes, 1916-1922' in Anne E O'Brien (ed.), *Studies in Irish, British and Australian Relations, 1916-1963: Trade, Diplomacy and Politics*, Four Courts Press, Dublin, 2005, pp. 27-39 at p. 31.
66 O'Brien, 'The Irish revolutionary movement', p. 33.
67 This paper focuses on the 1916 referendum. In 1917 an issue emerged which affected Catholics as Catholics, namely, the failure of the government to exempt teaching brothers and seminarians from being conscripted. That issue might have persuaded some Catholics, including Archbishop Michael Kelly, to switch from Yes to No as discussed in Kildea, 'Australian Catholics and conscription in the Great War'.
68 Kildea, *Tearing the Fabric*, pp. 179-180.

# Dr Herbert Michael ('Paddy') Moran: Catholic disruptor and contributor to Australian social history

## Anne Thoeming*

Although perhaps best known as a 'Wallabies' captain and cancer surgeon, Herbert Michael Moran had other achievements and was a man of contradictions. He was highly independent in his demeanour and inclined to dismiss the efforts of others he considered not aligned to his way of thinking, but cared deeply about those for whom life was a struggle. Although attesting that his Catholic faith never faltered, he nonetheless did not shy away from publicly criticising Catholics of all persuasions including priests and nuns. He was a prolific author of many professional and personal works, publishing his first memoir Viewless Winds in 1939.[1] It went to five editions partly due to the keen public interest generated by his comments about famous and somewhat infamous people alive at the time. The book received much publicity in the Australian and English press. It was considered to be richly entertaining and had wide appeal due to its breadth of coverage. Moran did not hesitate to share his own attitudes and opinions about institutions, events, colleagues and friends, and did so often in quite critical terms. His reflections of Australia and Australians give us an insight into the thinking of a somewhat disruptive Catholic.

Moran published three books about his life from 1885 to 1945 and these were all written after retirement. *Viewless Winds* was written and published while he was living in Europe and living apart from his wife and son. He was then 54 and perhaps felt the freedom to write from the heart, or maybe just to have his own voice. His books and other articles provide a highly subjective view of his agency as a writer and observer of Australian social and cultural history. These publications form the backdrop to Moran's life, and are artefacts which can be used by others to more objectively examine his actual historical legacy. His reputational impact was certainly highly contradictory. He is held in high esteem in Australian rugby history for his actions and behaviour as captain of the first Wallabies team tour of Britain, but his criticisms of people he knew and worked with earned him condemnation by some Church and medical colleagues. His success as a sportsman and medical professional is stark contrast with the reputation

* Anne Thoeming completed a Master of Research at Macquarie University in 2016. She is continuing her biographical investigation of Herbert Moran, and the ways he has informed historical knowledge of Australia and Australians. This article is refereed.

*Journal of the Australian Catholic Historical Society* 37-2 2016, 181-194 he developed as a critic of people and of the Church in Australia, as noted by historians such as Patrick O'Farrell and Edmund Campion, and his infatuation with Mussolini in the 1930s.[2]

It is in such contradictions that we start to see the benefits that historical biography can bring to telling the story of a life, and the story of relationships, of identity, and of representations within a life. There is much that can be said about Moran, especially when his life is considered within its historical context. He was deeply interested in the treatment and management of cancer which then, as now, was a significant public health issue. His circle of friends reflected a wide intellectual engagement, and he medically treated the poet and scholar Christopher Brennan. A staunch supporter of Britain in WW1 and pro-conscriptionist, he, too, felt the inner conflict that resonated with other Catholic and non-Catholic Irish middle-class Australians who supported conscription. Later, his fascination with European literature and all things Italian led him to make some significant life choices which were disruptive to his family. For a man whose working-class father arrived in Australia penniless, he has generated much intellectual interest within his spheres of influence, and he is still an enigma.

Although Moran has had some recognition as a figure of note in Australian social history, he is generally not widely known. A 1986 entry in the *Australian Dictionary of Biography* provides an overview of his life, and further information about him is included in a published family history journal article.[3] He is briefly mentioned in various institutional and sport history volumes as well as medical memoirs. He is also remembered by the Royal Australasian College of Surgeons for the medical history prize that was founded in his name.[4] These elements are bought together in the following story of Moran which discusses his life and some of his contributions, as well as his disruptions. It tells of a man who seemed to outgrow Australia far too soon; who realised too late that Australia was not such a bad place after all; and whose historical agency is yet to be fully revealed

Moran was born in 1885 as the third child of Michael and Annie Moran who had married in Sydney in 1881. Moran's Irish father arrived in Australia in 1877 at age 19 describing his occupation as "farm labourer", but forty years later as a bakery business owner he 'had the largest private business of its kind in the State'.[5] Moran's mother was Australian-born of Irish immigrants. She died at age 30 from birth-related septicaemia when Moran was just five. Although Moran's father ceased to practice his Catholic faith after his wife's death, the children were raised as Catholic and Moran attended Catholic schools – very briefly St Joseph's College at Hunters Hill, but mainly St Aloysius for his secondary schooling. Moran's family story is very much one of class transition and reflects the motif of progressive Irish Australians, both Protestant and Catholic, whose power and influence were disproportionate to their number.[6]

There are a few references to his university undergraduate days in his *Viewless Winds* memoir, but one important element stands out – especially in relation to his later life. Moran saw himself as an outsider, both physically and socially, when he commenced at the University of Sydney. Describing himself as a 'miserable, stooped, poring, introspective sort of fellow in my third year at the University' he nevertheless decided to take up an opportunity offered by a family friend to play a game of rugby, but this was not with the University.[7] The Rose Bay Football Club instead provided him with his first rugby experience and the chance to play with ordinary people and to no purpose aside from enjoyment and competitive spirit. Being a member of the team gave him a sense of belonging and seemed to meet an inner need for acceptance and recognition. At the end of football season celebrations, the Club gave him an honour cap for forward play, and reflecting back some 36 years later, he acknowledged the sense of pride he felt at receiving the award. He was clearly successful at this sport and five years later captained the first Australian rugby team to tour England.

Moran graduated from the University of Sydney in medicine in 1907 and then worked as a General Practitioner in Newcastle where he continued to play rugby. In 1908, he captained a strong Newcastle team in a match against an equally strong Sydney team, and the team won. The win caught the attention of Australian tour selectors who appointed him to the team, and later made him captain of the inaugural Australian rugby tour of Britain in 1908/1909.[8] The tour marked the first use of the 'Wallabies' name and the first time that Australia had defeated Britain in an international Rugby tour. According to Moran, it was suggested that the name 'Rabbits' be adopted by the team when it arrived in Plymouth, but the team rejected it in favour of name Wallabies, of which Moran said 'some of the local Devon people could not pronounce correctly'.[9] Moran took his responsibilities for leading these young men seriously. The four to six week voyage travelling first class on the R.M.S. *Omrah* enabled Moran to utilise his medical training and educate his team mates about team tactics and medical matters. Prior to arriving in Colombo, he took advantage of the opportunity to inform the men about the transmission modes and effects of syphilis using a medical text book he had taken on board which contained some rather graphic images. Later, he proudly noted that during the five month tour 'not one of the thirty-one players contracted venereal disease' and counted this as a real achievement.[10] Although he was confident about this fact, this statement also says something about Moran's tendency to embellish stories, a characteristic noted later by his medical peers.

The tour was a success for Australia and the first time the British international team had suffered such a defeat at the hands of Australia, but the win came at a social and reputational cost. The sports historian Tony Collins describes the tour as 'dogged by controversy and deteriorating relations with their British host. The Scottish and Irish rugby unions refused to play them because of suspicions that the Australians were professionals. On the field, the tourists were accused of being violent and playing solely for the purpose of winning'.[11] Equally, the British were accused of blatant hostility both on the field, and in the press. However, sports writer Spiro Zavos notes that despite these circumstances and throughout these matches, Moran set the standard for the expectations of the role of the captain, and that this standard 'created the template of a Wallaby captain throughout the twentieth century'.[12]

Injury forced Moran from some of the matches and contributed to his decision to leave the team and stay in Britain to undertake two years of postgraduate medical training, mostly in Edinburgh and London. He returned to Australia in 1910 and in 1914, married Eva Everil Augusta Mann. Eva was from a family of wealthy Sydney hoteliers, albeit from an Irish convict background. The family had owned Petty's Hotel, a once historic landmark of Sydney located at 1 York Street. Sadly, their family life was tragically marked by the deaths of five of their six children due to Rhesus disease. The strain of this, as well as Moran's frequent travels overseas, contributed to a difficult and disrupted family life and perhaps contributed to their later separation.

Moran enlisted for war service in 1915 and the vivid descriptions of his time operating at sea on the war wounded are chilling. He provides some insight into a world that from a medical perspective was forever changed. A well-stocked drug cabinet to assist the dying quickly became a thing of the past, and the respectful farewell to a deceased was quickly substituted by a swift, silent burial at sea. Moran's comment that 'in war, the dead shame always those who survive' reveals a depth of feeling about the role and impact of war.[13] He described the operating theatre where he and others worked as comprising a narrow fixed table in the dispensary of a co-opted cattle freighter. Moran's war descriptions received praise in a *Times Literary*

*Supplement* review published in London. The review acknowledged Moran's literary gift, and also his forthrightness in describing the ignorant and unscrupulous behaviour of some of the doctors in his book – particularly those with drug and alcohol problems.

The *Times* review finishes with a quotation from Viewless Winds which reflects Moran's thinking on the role and responsibilities of medical practitioners, and medical engagement with patients:

> 'In wars we have faced dagger and lance, sword and musket. The missiles change, but we have not changed. We have stood the shock of every epidemic, going forth to meet the terror of a new disease armoured only in the tradition of service. We remained in cities which half the people had deserted; and not as cowards or plunderers. If we were paid, we were not always mercenaries. When the dead were put outside, like garbage tins, our bodies were there, too'.[14]

Moran's time at war was cut short owing to the dysentery he contracted, and which continued to plague him. He returned to Australia in 1916 and 'found Australia in the throes of a miserable sectarian brawl'[15] He was a middle-class Catholic who supported conscription, unlike Church leaders such as the very vocal and highly influential Archbishop Daniel Mannix who stridently opposed conscription. Moran's support for conscription was based on his belief that 'those who share the privileges of peace in a State should bear equally the burden of war'.[16] It was also informed by his medical experience at war, and related concerns about war mortality. He believed that conscription would provide many more troops and accordingly, provide assurance that sufficient reinforcements could be available on the western front in France to cover those injured and needing time to recover.

The widespread opposition in the Church to conscription appalled Moran. Perhaps in his role as a doctor, he saw the adverse social and economic impact on everyday Catholics as sectarian influences inflamed the conscription debate, and he directly attributed this to Archbishop Mannix as a result of his public statements.

> 'It was a painful epoch for Catholic citizens; they became now the scapegoats for every social evil. In both the laity and the clergy a great gulf divided the two sections. Lukewarm Catholics publicly denied their faith. Many who didn't, became bitterly anti-clerical, speaking of some of their own priests with crude offensiveness. Doctor Mannix achieved nothing more than a notoriety which seemed strangely gratifying to his austere mind.....He penalised severely the poorer Catholics and the little Catholic tradesmen. He caused social ostracism of the professional Catholics'.[17]

In 1921 and while still suffering the effects of his wartime dysentery, Moran decided to spend some time in Europe with his family. Sailing with him to England was Father Maurice O'Reilly, Rector of St. John's College at the University of Sydney. O'Reilly was representing New South Wales at the Irish Race Congress and invited Moran to act similarly for Tasmania, which did not have a representative. Gladly accepting the invitation, Moran described his participation at the Congress as insignificant, although he was a member of a sub-committee which included Eamon de Valera, the President of the Irish Republic. Moran didn't describe the exact purpose of the sub-committee but he did note that De Valera's reports of its findings never quite tallied with his recollections and in general, de Valera seemed intent upon achieving his own ends, rather than representing the Free State Government which was paying his way. In all, Moran thought little of the Congress and described it as more like a 'well-organised social event'.[18] Despite this, he was somewhat captivated by some of the attendees. He probably had never met people like this before and Mary MacSwiney was one who drew his attention. She was a Sinn Fein member and leader whose brother Terence had died in a hunger strike in 1920. Moran describes how she never once smiled during the Congress and her 'speech was a scalding infusion from all the bitter herbs that ever grew in the crevices of suffering and misfortune'.[19]

When back in Australia, Moran concentrated more of his professional time on the treatment of cancer, particularly cervical cancer in women. This interest led him to undertake research into its causes and incidence, and to travel overseas, which not surprisingly was disruptive to his family life. Australian cancer research was then essentially laboratory-based so, as a cancer practitioner, Moran's clinical observations and interpretations of the work being undertaken were significant. In those early days, clinic and hospital treatment for cancer patients was minimal and treatment mostly experimental. Moran was the first in Australia to trial the surgical use of radium needles in the treatment of cancer. This method involved the insertion of the needles into tumour sites rather than more general radiation treatment or site surgery. He purchased his own radium supply on a visit to America in 1922 and carried the radium around in a lead container in his hip pocket.

Although he was well aware of the dangers posed by radium exposure, the extent of its power and impact was not then fully appreciated. However, Moran soon became concerned that insufficient attention was being paid to patient management, and noted that the lack of clinical protocols around the use of radium was also causing problems for both doctors and patients. It wasn't until much later, in 1927/28, that the Commonwealth Government responded to these concerns and commenced purchasing centralised supplies and working with State medical authorities to implement protocols around the distribution and use of radium. Prior to this period, Canberra's responsibility was limited to contributing money to individual institutions for the conduct of their own cancer research work.[20]

Moran became a member of the Cancer Research Committee based within the University of Sydney and used his position to argue for better cancer treatment and patient management. This passion for improved cancer treatment was fuelled by his experiences with cancer patients. The descriptions of his patients and their reception of his diagnosis, as well as the everyday challenges to doctors in diagnosing, informing and treating patients, the despair they felt with this work, the patient experience of the physical transformations resulting from the disease, including the smell of cancer in patients in their final stages, are powerful writing.

These descriptions and those of his experience with this Committee provides historical insight into the management of cancer research in Australia. Dr Henry Chapman was the Committee Director and Moran tells how he became increasingly concerned about Chapman's management style and research competency. Although he had an earlier promising academic career, Chapman was considered by Moran to have dubious research abilities and suspect moral integrity.[21] Information about how he neglected his duties, misappropriated public research funds and later, following the threat of suspension, committed suicide were then confined within the close University and Committee community. Moran's telling of these events in *Viewless Winds* brought the story to a bigger, more public audience, and his indignation that University management was trying to cover-up this embarrassing campus moment is palpable in his book. He felt the University wanted to avoid adverse publicity and hushed up the misconduct of Henry Chapman and the concerns with Committee operations. Moran made his case in *Viewless Winds* saying 'what still perplexes me is this: That any university could have entrusted the direction of research work to a man whose integrity they already suspected'.[22] Although Moran's own reputation within the Faculty of Medicine suffered because of his general tendency to freely criticise colleagues in print and in person, in the matter of the Cancer Research Committee his insider view of this debacle is historically valuable because it gives voice to otherwise silent events, and brought to the surface some uncomfortable truths.[23] Today the University acknowledges the story of Chapman and the Committee as 'one of ultimate disgrace'.[24]

Although professionally focussed on his medical career, Moran maintained a wide network of acquaintances across different interest areas, and was involved in numerous Catholic medical activities, partly aided by the connections of his wife. Eva was the twin of Furneaux Mann who, like Moran, was a member of the French dining-club, Les Compliqués, where members spoke only in French. Eva's in-laws included the Catholic doctors Walter Burfitt, and Mary Burfitt-Williams, one of the first three women to achieve first class honours at the University of Sydney medical school.[25] Moran was a founding member of the Medical Guild of St Luke, a network of Catholic doctors which met to discuss and share information about the teachings of the Church as they related to the practice of medicine. He was a prolific contributor to professional publications, especially the Medical Journal of Australia. While most articles related to cancer treatments and innovations, his keen interest in medical history was clearly evident in the range of his writing.

A passionate interest in European languages, literature and culture was ultimately transformative for Moran and was reflected in his frequent travels to Europe – at least eight times in his life. He met Mussolini several times in the 1930s and was thanked by Mussolini for his work to 'initiate the University teaching of Italian in Sydney'.[26] The exact motivation for Moran's embrace of Mussolini and fascism is unclear, and he was like other foreigners in Italy who, according to historian Roslyn Pesman Cooper, 'succumbed to Mussolini's well-manipulated personal magnetism'.[27] Pesman Cooper notes that Moran 'became a publicist and propagandist for Italy' in his many efforts to promote Italy and Italian culture, and worked to foster improved relations between Italy and Britain with a view to minimising the risks of an increasing German influence in Italy in the lead-up to World War 2.

Moran's positive views of Mussolini were not inconsistent with earlier Australian Catholic views, and reflected a satisfaction with the social transformation of Italy under the dictator and closer political association with the Vatican. On his return from Rome in 1930, Archbishop Kelly of Sydney said in an interview with the *Sydney Morning Herald*:

> Mussolini had restored order out of chaos. There was no unemployment, and, although many of the people lived frugally, they were contented. 'If we had in Australia a Mussolini who knew how to give effect to his conclusions,' said Dr. Kelly, 'we would have no unemployment, we would have land made available, and every man would be required

## Dr Herbert Michael ('Paddy') Moran

to fulfil his duties, whether workman or employer. We would have no supernumeraries. We would have the needs of the country supplied by national produce".[28]

This passion for Italy drove him to live there after his retirement from medicine in 1935, and he stayed until the outbreak of WW2. His memoir and other writing reveals his intense dissatisfaction with the inward looking nation Australia had become during this period, and said of Australia that 'In their excitements and their pursuits they wished to shut their eyes to the clouds gathering a long way away'.[29] His first few months in Italy were writing a series of letters which were later compiled and published in 1935 under the title *Letters from Rome*.[30] The *Letters* were directed to an Australian audience and served as an apologia for Mussolini and an attack on the treatment of Italy by the League of Nations following Italy's invasion of Abyssinia. The six letters focused on post-war international events, fleshed out with items of significance to Australia.

Following the outbreak of WW2 and feeling he had more to contribute, he re-joined the Royal Army Medical Corps ultimately working as President of Medical Boards in Colchester England.[31] In 1945 he was diagnosed with a malignant melanoma, and while dying took the opportunity to craft a narrative of his death march and published this description in his final publication *In My Fashion*.[32] He died in Cambridge where he is buried.

With a complex personal life, Moran's publications provide a glimpse into a middle-class professional life where marriages broke down, children died, and scandals erupted. Little is directly revealed by Moran in his memoirs about his family and his other personal arrangements although he was particularly close to the Fiaschi family, and deeply valued his long friendship with Dr H M Molesworth, who kept some of Moran's letters now held in the NSW State Library, Sydney. Historian Hermione Lee notes of biographical subjects 'they speak, they change, they grow old, and they die', but there is a sense of poignancy and also intrigue in the great silence about Moran's personal life.[33] The *Australian National Review* commented on the absence of his wife from any recollections, and the sense that 'tragedy seems to lurk somewhere between the lines'.[34]

Faith rather than religiosity seemed more important to Moran, and he was guided by a strong sense of inner belief rather than attachment to the Church. His writings are infused positively with faith references and somewhat more negatively with references to Church politics particularly in matters of conscription and morality. Misbehaving priests and nuns were an easy target and he was accused of being anti-clerical. He did not object to the Church's engagement with social action and believed that priests did too little to implement *Quadragesimo Anno*. Using the example of one unnamed priest, he wrote 'what had he ever done to implement in a poor suburb the wise counsels of *Quadragesimo Anno*... though we have a Catholic system of social justice, few of our leaders expound it'.[35]

His openness in criticising behaviour he considered incompatible with religious life was consistent with his belief that rules and laws should be obeyed; that ordinary Catholics struggling to obey the tenets of the faith had the right to expect nuns and priests to model good behaviour; that celibacy was too difficult and clergy should be allowed to marry. He was not tolerant of those holding the reins of power and who exercised it irresponsibly, and his criticisms of named and unnamed Catholics led to a sense that he was more organisationally outside the tent than inside it. When published, the description of one Mother Superior, whom he considered to be 'very conscious of her exalted position ... she wore an air of exaggerated humility, masterfully', and description of others who 'move about fastidiously like masks in a religious spectacle, scenting the applause of the onlookers, too often keenly aware of their own haloes', counted as a deep betrayal of his Church.[36] In reply his Catholic medical colleagues fought back with a strong rejection of his 'unworthy aspersions upon a class of women of whom any religion and any country might well be proud'.[37]

The impact in Australia of these and other comments in *Viewless Winds* were considered inflammatory to the Church, medical peers and a small number of others too. John Preece, the editor of *Desiderata*, said that despite Moran reaching 'one of the highest positions in his profession in this country, where he was born' he lets everyone down through his criticisms of the people and the institutions that have allowed him to achieve so much.[38] Preece considered the chapter on patient revelations to be 'a sore place in the book...the cases are known to the doctor and to the priest, each in his own confessional, and beyond that they need not go'.[39]

What drove Moran to these views and sentiments is an area for further exploration. He always held in high regard those he considered to be models of a Catholic life, and seemed sympathetic to those who were all too aware of their personal failings and inability to meet the expectations of a consecrated life. It is likely that Moran's medical experiences as well as his exposure to different thinking through a wider network of Catholic and non-Catholic people. Both in Australia and elsewhere, gave him an insight into aspects of his religion that may well have fuelled an increasing sense of conflict with the Australian Church – conflict over religious rites that he saw as impositions of a dominant Irish clergy disconnected from an increasingly secular society.

Regardless of what he said or did, Moran was a great networker across many areas and perhaps this in some way explains the ongoing fascination with him. Part of the attraction of Moran as a biographical subject is not only his achievements, transgressions or legacies – his life from cradle to the grave - but rather the voice he gave to the everyday people populating his narratives. We can hear part of their stories through his works and understand more about their lives in a way that was simply not possible otherwise. Part of the reason for this is his refusal to be limited by, or exclude, the confessional, private stories given to doctors and priests. He symbolically changed the Australian Catholic Church narrative because his people-based view was from the pew.

Moran provided a different and more critical style of thinking about the Church and its influence – it was more outsider than insider. The Catholic Weekly obituary of Moran said 'Outside of his own Church he was accepted and respected as an uncompromising, devout, and if need arose, a militant Catholic'.[40] However, it asked people to remember his 'unbounded charity to, and consideration for, those of scanty resources in the course of his social and professional relationships'.[41] *The Bulletin's* review of *Viewless Winds* contains what can be viewed as a quintessential leitmotif of Moran's approach. It says 'He brings the religious mind to medicine, a doctor's mind to the consideration of religion'.[42]

## Bibliography

B M 'Viewless Winds', *Australian National Review* 6, no. 31 (July 1939).

Campion, Edmund. *Australian Catholic Lives.* Kew East Victoria: David Lovell Publishing, 2014.

Collins, Tony, 'The Tyranny of Deference: Anglo–Australian Relations and Rugby Union before World War II.' *Sport in History* 29, no. 3 (2009): 437-56.

'Death of Eminent Surgeon.' *The Catholic Weekly*, 29 November 1945.

Finnane, Mark, 'The English Have No Altruism: J V Barry and Irish Identity in Twentieth Century Australia.' [In English]. *History Australia* 4, no. 2 (2007).

Health, Director-General of, 'Report of the Second Australian Cancer Conference.' Canberra, 1931.

'An Interview,' *Sydney Morning Herald (NSW: 1842-1954)*, 10 October 1930, 11.

J L P 'Dr. Moran's Restless Violence.' *Desiderata*, no. 40 (May 1939): 3.

Lee, Hermione. *Biography: A Very Short Introduction.* Very Short Introductions, Oxford: Oxford University Press, 2009.

Letter to His Grace the Most Reverend N T Gilroy, D D, From the Catholic Medical Guild of St. Luke. 15 May 1939.

Moran, Herbert, M, *In My Fashion: An Autobiography of the Last Ten Years.* London: Peter Davies, 1946.

Moran, Herbert, M, *Letters from Rome: An Australian's View of the Italo-Abyssinian Question.* Sydney: Angus & Robertson, 1935.

Moran, Herbert, M, *Viewless Winds: Being the Recollections and Digressions of an Australian Surgeon.* London: Peter Davies, 1939.

Moran, M P A, 'Irish and Australian', *Offaly Heritage: Journal of the Offaly Historical and Archaeological Society* 5 (2007-2008): 20.

O'Farrell, Patrick. *The Catholic Church and Community: An Australian History.* Revised Edition ed. Kensington: New South Wales University Press, 1985.

Pesman Cooper, Roslyn, 'An Australian in Mussolini's Italy; Herbert Michael Moran', *Overland*, no. 115 (1989).

Pollard, Jack, *Australian Rugby: The Game and the Players*, Chippendale: Pan Macmillan, 1994.

'The Red Page: Irishmen at Large', *The Bulletin*, 18 May 1939.

Sydney University, 'Chapman, Henry George,' University of Sydney, sydney.edu.au/medicine/museum/mwmuseum/index.php/Chapman_Henry_George.

Walsh, G P, 'Moran, Herbert Michael (1885-1945),' *Australian Dictionary of Biography*, 576-77: Australian National University, 1986.

Webb, Nina, and John Atherton Young, 'The Medical School in the 1920s', *Centenary Book of the University of Sydney Faculty of Medicine*, edited by John Atherton Young, Ann Jervie Sefton and Nina Webb. Sydney: Sydney University Press, 1984, chap. 5.

Zavos, Spiro. *Golden Wallabies: The Story of Australia's Rugby World Champions*, Ringwood: Penguin Books, 2000.

## Notes

1. Herbert M Moran, *Viewless Winds: Being the Recollections and Digressions of an Australian Surgeon*, London: Peter Davies, 1939.
2. Patrick O'Farrell, *The Catholic Church and Community: An Australian History*, Revised Edition ed. Kensington: New South Wales University Press, 1985; Edmund Campion, *Australian Catholic Lives*, Kew East Victoria: David Lovell Publishing, 2014.
3. G P. Walsh, 'Moran, Herbert Michael (1885-1945),' in *Australian Dictionary of Biography* (Australian National University, 1986). Accessed 1 January 2017. M P A Moran, 'Irish and Australian,' *Offaly Heritage: Journal of the Offaly Historical and Archaeological Society* 5 (2007-2008).
4. http://www.surgeons.org/member-services/scholarships-awards-lectures-prizes/lectures-and-prizes/ accessed 1 January 2017.
5. Moran, *Viewless Winds: Being the Recollections and Digressions of an Australian Surgeon*, 8.
6. Mark Finnane explores this in further detail in his article on J V Barry, Mark Finnane, "'The English Have No Altruism': J V Barry and Irish Identity in Twentieth Century Australia," *History Australia* 4, no. 2 (2007), 41, 9.
7. Moran, *Viewless Winds: Being the Recollections and Digressions of an Australian Surgeon*, 33.
8. Jack Pollard, *Australian Rugby: The Game and the Players*, Chippendale: Pan Macmillan, 1994.
9. Moran, *Viewless Winds: Being the Recollections and Digressions of an Australian Surgeon*, 63.
10. Ibid, 63.
11. Tony Collins, 'The Tyranny of Deference: Anglo–Australian Relations and Rugby Union before World War II,' *Sport in History* 29, no. 3 (2009), 440-441.
12. Spiro Zavos, *Golden Wallabies: The Story of Australia's Rugby World Champions*, Ringwood: Penguin Books, 2000,107.
13. Moran, *Viewless Winds: Being the Recollections and Digressions of an Australian Surgeon*, 137.
14. Ibid, 319.
15. Ibid, 155.
16. Ibid, 175.
17. Ibid, 158-159.
18. Ibid, 196.
19. Ibid, 191.
20. Director-General of Health, 'Report of the Second Australian Cancer Conference,' (Canberra, 1931).

21 Nina Webb and John Atherton Young, 'The Medical School in the 1920s,' in *Centenary Book of the University of Sydney Faculty of Medicine*, ed. John Atherton Young, Ann Jervie Sefton, and Nina Webb, Sydney: Sydney University Press, 1984.
22 Moran, *Viewless Winds: Being the Recollections and Digressions of an Australian Surgeon*, 285.
23 Webb and Young, 'The Medical School in the 1920s.'
24 University of Sydney, 'Chapman, Henry George,' University of Sydney, sydney.edu.au/medicine/museum/mwmuseum/index.php/Chapman_Henry_George. accessed 30 December 2016.
25 Webb and Young, 'The Medical School in the 1920s.'
26 Herbert M Moran, *In My Fashion: An Autobiography of the Last Ten Years*, London: Peter Davies, 1946, 3.
27 Roslyn Pesman Cooper, 'An Australian in Mussolini's Italy; Herbert Michael Moran,' *Overland*, no. 115 (1989), 45.
28 'An Interview,' *Sydney Morning Herald* (NSW: 184–1954), 10 October 1930, 11.
29 Moran, *In My Fashion: An Autobiography of the Last Ten Years*, 36.
30 *Letters from Rome: An Australian's View of the Italo-Abyssinian Question*, Sydney: Angus & Robertson, 1935.
31 Moran, 'Irish and Australian.'
32 Moran, *In My Fashion: An Autobiography of the Last Ten Years*.
33 Hermione Lee, *Biography: A Very Short Introduction*, Very Short Introductions, Oxford: Oxford University Press, 2009, 4.
34 B M, 'Viewless Winds,' *Australian National Review* 6, no. 31 (1939), 83.
35 Moran, *Viewless Winds: Being the Recollections and Digressions of an Australian Surgeon*, 340.
36 Ibid, 215 and 343.
37 Letter to His Grace the Most Reverend N T Gilroy, D D, From the Catholic Medical Guild of St. Luke, 15 May 1939.
38 J L P, 'Dr. Moran's Restless Violence,' *Desiderata*, no. 40 (1939), 15.
39 Ibid, 17.
40 'Death of Eminent Surgeon,' *The Catholic Weekly*, 29 November 1945, 5.
41 Ibid, 5.
42 'The Red Page: Irishmen at Large,' *The Bulletin*, 18 May 1939, 2.

# The Pope's Peace Note of 1917: The British Response

## Youssef Taouk*

One hundred years ago, while the First World War was still raging in 1917, Pope Benedict XV sought to end the conflagration that had enveloped Europe through a negotiated peace. The Pope's Peace Note, as it became known, was issued in August 1917 and followed various other exhortations by Pope Benedict throughout the war. This article will suggest that the Pope's Peace Note was unsuccessful for two reasons: The first is that a negotiated peace such as the Pope advocated was looked upon as inadequate by the warring parties and so his initiative was cold-shouldered by civil governments, particularly in Britain. The second reason is that, for their part, a considerable number of British Catholics and their Catholic leaders paid mere lip-service to the peace utterances of their Pontiff publicly and at times the majority of Catholics in Britain expressed disagreement with the Pope's peace efforts, in particular the Pope's Peace Note of 1917.

Pius X, who was pope at the outbreak of the conflict in 1914, died on 20 August 1914, less than three weeks after the commencement of war. On 3 September Giacomo Della Chiesa, the Cardinal Archbishop of Bologna, was elected Pope. He adopted the name Benedict XV. Della Chiesa's essential training had been in diplomacy and he was an expert in jurisprudence,[1] and this made him well qualified to cope with the war.

Immediately upon his election to the Supreme Pontificate, Pope Benedict XV began toiling to halt the explosion that had absorbed Europe and work in the interest of a negotiated peace. Unlike other Catholic prelates who depicted it as a just war, he rejected the conflict as totally unjustifiable. Seen in this light, it is understandable that only two days after his coronation, the Pope issued a message in which he appealed for a negotiated peace. In this first message, he urged the belligerent leaders to solve their differences by diplomatic means and implored them "to reflect that this mortal life is already attended with enough misery and suffering as it is."[2]

Less than two months after this first appeal, Benedict XV issued his much anticipated first encyclical letter, *Ad Beatissimi Apostolorum*,[3] on 1 November 1914. In the encyclical, Benedict proceeded to list the causes of the war. He then renewed his call for the rulers of the warring nations to resolve their differences without resorting to arms.[4] Thus, Pope Benedict

---

* Dr Youssef Taouk is a research associate and lecturer at the Institute for Advancing Community Engagement at the Australian Catholic University in Sydney.

was an advocate of a negotiated settlement to the war from the very start.

But arms were not laid aside and the war continued unabated. Benedict was greatly disappointed at the failure of his encyclical to produce any fruit. In his first Christmas Eve allocution to the cardinals, he told them that he had hoped "to pierce this darkness of warring death with at least a ray, one single ray of the divine sun of peace."[5] The Pope, however, was not discouraged by his failure to end the conflict. A few weeks after he issued his first encyclical, on 10 January 1915, Cardinal Gasparri, the Vatican Secretary of State, published the details of a prayer for peace that had been prepared by Benedict XV. A letter was sent to the Catholic hierarchy throughout the world by Gasparri, instructing them that it was the Holy Father's wish that every church should dedicate the Mass to peace and the Pope's prayer for peace was ordered to be recited in all churches for the duration of the war.[6]

However, the governments, and by implication peoples, of Europe were not yet ready to listen to any talk of peace. Some Catholics among the Allies were so anxious to be accounted full patriots as to baulk at the encyclical.[7] They would have preferred that the Pope declare himself for a victory to the Allies (France, Britain, Russia and Italy) or to the Central Powers (Germany, Austria-Hungary and Turkey) instead, depending on which side they were.

In Britain, most of the Catholic press declared its support for *Ad Beatissimi*, with the *Catholic Times* welcoming it as a refreshing document.[8] In contrast, leading British Catholics voiced their view that the time was not propitious to support peace in the months following the Pope's prayer for peace.[9] The opinion was prevalent among British Catholics, as among many pro-war commentators, that a peace at that time with an undefeated Germany would be premature and nothing more than a blueprint for a larger, more destructive future war. In April 1915, *The Tablet*, the conservative Catholic weekly, fully endorsed the views that "Peace to-day could be no more than an armed truce, a pretence, a hypocrisy."[10] The danger of a hasty peace was further emphasised by Hilaire Belloc, the pre-eminent Catholic author in Britain. On 30 April, a little over a month after the Pope's prayer was ordered to be recited in Catholic churches throughout the world, Belloc delivered a lecture in Liverpool in which he warned that if the Allies were duped into accepting peace terms, "it would be equivalent to the signing of the death-warrant of Great Britain."[11]

There were Catholics who genuinely supported the Pope's calls for peace. The Jesuits for example, were in the forefront of Benedict's supporters and Sydney Smith, a Jesuit priest, was among the most ardent defenders of the Pope's peace efforts. He published an article in *The Month*, the Catholic monthly journal, in January 1915, soon after *Ad Beatissimi* was issued, with a positive explanation of what the encyclical contained.[12]

Despite the failure of his appeals to the powers to solve international problems by arbitration rather than by resorting to the might of arms, Benedict was determined to "Cry out, cease not".[13] His next peace pronouncement, *Allorchè Fummo*, the Apostolic Exhortation to the Belligerent Peoples and Their Rulers, was issued on 28 July 1915, one year after the commencement of war. In his Exhortation, he implored the leaders of the belligerents to end the carnage and reminded them of the responsibility that they were endowed with.[14] An incredibly accurate prophecy followed this impassioned plea. Benedict warned the hostile peoples of the dire consequences if vanquished nations were subjected to a humiliating peace: "nations do not die; humbled and oppressed they chafe under the yoke imposed upon them, preparing a renewal of the conflict, and passing down from generation to generation a mournful heritage of hatred and revenge."[15] This remarkable prophecy put the case clearly for a negotiated peace as a better outcome.

Although British Catholics tried to display public support for the peace proposal, in effect it was received with a marked coolness that amounted to a rebuff. The Catholic press, while attempting to show at least some solidarity with Benedict's peace appeal, implicitly rejected the kind of peace that he was advocating. Although the *Catholic Times* expressed gratitude to the Pontiff for his peace effort, it frankly admitted that this was not the proper moment to pursue peace.[16] The Universe, traditionally an ardent defender of Catholicism, showed an amazing lack of diplomacy in rejecting the Pope's peace appeal. *The Universe* warned outright that short of a Prussian victory, a colossal disaster would befall the Entente if they concluded peace at that moment.[17]

Privately, eminent Catholics were even less inclined to accept a peace similar to that proposed by Benedict XV. It seems that the concept of an allegedly "inconclusive peace" continued to plague them, and it was widely accepted that if peace came in 1915, Britain might have to fight a better prepared Germany in the near future.[18] The British Catholic hierarchy advocated a peace with victory. While there is no evidence in the private papers of the episcopacy to indicate what they thought of Benedict's peace initiative, one may confidently deduce that they did not receive it favourably from the lack of utterances in support of Benedict's effort at that time. This inference is further buttressed by the numerous pastorals and sermons in which the hierarchy implored their people to pray for a victorious peace.[19]

The number of British Catholics who remained truly loyal to Benedict's principles of peace and reconciliation dwindled to an astonishingly small minority. The lack of support for a Pope's peace among the majority of British Catholics can be discerned in their antagonism to a small *ad hoc* Catholic organisation which promoted quite specifically the precise formula for peace advocated by Benedict. The skillfully named Guild of the Pope's Peace[20] was founded by Francis Meynell and Stanley Morison, two Catholic pacifists, after the introduction of conscription in Britain in January 1916. The Guild was composed of a committee of seven people, including two priests, which made up its limited membership. In a "Preliminary Notice", issued in early 1916, the Guild explained that the Pope had invited "all the friends of peace in the world to help Us in hastening the end of the war."[21] The Notice called on every loyal Catholic to answer Benedict's pleas in order for them to be effective.

Most of the British Catholic bishops, while not condemning the Guild publicly, disapproved of it privately. Evidence suggests that this reached the highest level of authority in the British Catholic Church. Cardinal Francis Bourne, the nominal leader of the Catholic hierarchy in Britain, wrote to the Catholic Duke of Norfolk, who was a peer in the House of Lords, telling him that the Guild had no authorization of any kind.[22] This opposition to the Guild from the Catholic hierarchy reveals one of the great paradoxes of the war from the British Catholic perspective. The hierarchical authorities, entrusted with promoting the Pope's ideals by the Church itself, became staunch opponents of the Guild of the Pope's Peace because it did not fit the "patriotic" image of the British Catholic community.[23] The Guild's influence gradually faded away as the majority of Catholics remained firmly entrenched in the "patriotic" camp. Isolating the Guild and stifling its voice would convince the wider British public, which was already accusing Catholics of disloyalty (in the context of the Irish Easter Uprising of 1916), that the Guild was not representative of Catholic opinion.

Up to 1917, the Pope's peace utterances had been merely acknowledged politely or ignored by the great powers. In the first half of 1917, however, signs of the growing desire for peace among the warring people of Europe were beginning to show. In March, the first Russian Revolution took place, and the Petrograd Soviet announced that its policy was to seek a negotiated peace under the formula of "no annexations, no indemnities"; in May, the French army mutinied after the failure of the Nivelle offensive. More importantly, in July the German Reichstag devised and passed the Peace

Resolution demanding that the government renounce annexations and support a peace of understanding.[24]

This intensifying popular pressure in favour of a moderate peace prompted the Vatican to embark on an adventure in peace diplomacy. In July 1917, Pope Benedict drafted a note offering concrete proposals for peace. The Pope's Peace Note, one of the most significant attempts to end the conflict during the First World War, was issued on 10 August 1917.[25] The Note was more practical and precise in its proposals than any other peace initiative that had hitherto been published. The proposals of the Note can be summarised in seven main points:

1) the substitution of material force with "the moral force of law";
2) simultaneous and reciprocal disarmament;
3) a mutual commitment to international arbitration;
4) true freedom "and common use" of the seas;
5) mutual renunciation of all war indemnities;
6) restoration of all occupied territories;
7) the examination of disputed territorial claims in a "spirit of equity and justice".

In Germany, there was strong opposition to the Peace Note from right-wing newspapers and leading Protestants.[26] In addition, these newspapers resented the fact that the Pope had chosen the jubilee year of the Reformation to inspire a negotiated peace.

In Britain, France, and Italy it was claimed that the Pope's Peace Note was German-inspired. In Britain, the government received the Note with suspicion and accused the Vatican of being in constant contact with the Germans while composing the proposals. As a result, according to British government sources, the terms of the proposals were of a greater benefit to the Central Powers than to the Allies.[27] The Foreign Office minutes at the time of the Note's reception indicate the immense suspicion with which it was viewed. One official referred to the Pope's Note as a "thoroughly pro-German document".[28]

The British government was in a predicament. If the Central Powers accepted the Pope's proposals, then Britain could not be seen to reject them outright. So, initially, it was decided that the British government should send an acknowledgement and await developments. On 21 August 1917, Arthur Balfour, the British Foreign Secretary, telegraphed a message acknowledging the Pope's Peace Note and informing the Vatican that the British Government had not yet had a chance to consult its Allies.[29] This was to be the only official reply that the Vatican was to receive from Britain regarding the Peace Note.

With the exception of some Radicals and pacifists, the peace proposals were received with hostility and vehement criticism in Britain.[30] The "fight-to-the-finish" press, in particular, swiftly dismissed the proposals as propitious for Germany and disadvantageous to Great Britain. The Anglican *Guardian* dismissed the peace terms curtly, positing that "no Allied Government will give them five minutes' serious consideration...."[31] On 16 August, *The Times* labeled the initiative "pro-German and...anti-Ally" and accused Benedict of offering "a German peace".[32]

The Pope's own flock in Britain viewed the Note with some discomfort. Most prominent British Catholics were not yet ready to support a negotiated peace but could not reject outright their Pontiff's peace offer – the most notable peace move yet offered in the three years of war. Thus, in a show of solidarity with their Pontiff, they publicly welcomed the Pope's attempt to procure peace for a dying Europe and defended the move as the Pope's duty.

The British Catholic press mounted a campaign in defence of the Note and while some Catholic organs were careful not to endorse it, others affirmed their loyalty by attempting to vindicate it. They were simply doing their duty in justifying the Peace Note in the face of what they considered to be a bigoted and intolerant environment. Having said this, however, it must be noted that not all Catholic newspapers welcomed the substance of the Peace Note and some even showed public reserve in accepting it. *The Tablet*, for example, while approving some of the terms proposed by the Pope, rejected the Note in no uncertain terms. It argued that moral justice was alien to the German ideal of *Kultur*. It was only fair, *The Tablet* continued, that the Peace Note be judged on the assumption that the Allies could not attain complete victory. But such an assumption, the paper added, was not shared by the British "and certainly not by anyone connected with this journal."[33]

*The Tablet* earned a reprimand from some Catholic newspapers for its imprudence and its lack of respect in dealing with the Note. The *Glasgow Observer* was one of those Catholic organs that chastised *The Tablet*, claiming that it had dealt "with the appeal of his Holiness in terms little less derogatory than those held by the other Jingo Tory organs."[34] However, in defending the Pope, the *Observer* assured the wider public that British Catholics were not disposed to embarrass the government in any moment of difficulty by making extreme judgements in the political field.[35] In this way, the *Glasgow Observer* at once retained its allegiance to the Holy See while at the same time professing its loyalty to the government.

The *Catholic Times* and the *Catholic Herald* welcomed the Pope's peace initiative wholeheartedly, the *Catholic Times* even declaring that the contents of the Note indicated that morally the Pope was on the Allies' side.[36] While urging the belligerents to give the Pope's proposals the utmost consideration, the *Catholic Herald* directed its appeal to Catholics especially. Catholics, it stressed, must throw their complete support behind the Pope so he would not be left isolated.[37]

Attempts to publicise the Peace Note and to show that it was issued from a position of impartiality were also disseminated through pamphlets and booklets written by prominent Catholics. One such widely disseminated pamphlet was the Jesuit priest, Fr Cyril Martindale's *The Pope's Peace Note*, published in September by the Catholic Social Guild. The pamphlet was sold out with astonishing speed.[38] In commenting on the Peace Note, Martindale explained that because he was Christ's representative on earth, the Pope could not be silent. Martindale warned that, just because the Note was a diplomatic rather than an ecclesiastical document, Catholics should not consider themselves free to dismiss it as unsatisfactory.[39]

In contrast to the public show of support for the Pope's Peace Note on the part of most of the Catholic press and the pamphleteers, the majority of leading Catholics were hesitant to accept the proposed terms at the expense of abandoning Britain's war aims. A determination to achieve peace through victory was in fact the reaction of Cardinal Bourne. Bourne publicly expressed his disagreement with the Pontiff's Peace Note and his commitment to British war aims when he declared, shortly after the Note was released:

> The Pope has proposed that all the belligerents should come to a compromise. No! We demand the total triumph of right over wrong. We do not want a peace which will be no more than a truce or armistice between two wars. There may be in our land some people who want peace at any price, but they have no following among us. We English Catholics are fully behind our war leaders.[40]

Speaking for his flock in England, Bourne had apparently either forgotten, or chose to ignore the minority of Catholic men and women who were part of the peace movement, especially the Guild of the Pope's Peace. Soon after Bourne's declaration, the Guild printed a booklet reviewing the history of Popes and peace and contradicting Bourne's confident assertion. The booklet enquired accusingly:

> How is it that even now, after the Pope's proposal of terms which would secure all the finer objects for which our politicians claimed

to be fighting, and for which the masses of our soldiers are indeed fighting, there are many Catholics who still reject the Holy Father's mediation? Not only do they reject it, but...seeking to invent new 'war aims' when the old are in danger of realisation, many endure in silence, some even approve, the calumnies of the war press against the Holy Father.[41]

This stark contradiction, which clearly showed that not all Catholics were fully behind their war leaders, must surely have disconcerted Bourne. It also demonstrates a key reason behind the hierarchy's determination to denounce the Guild.

Nevertheless, Bourne's blatant repudiation of the Pope's peace offer must have been very satisfying for the opponents of Benedict XV. One can imagine how justified they would have felt at the sight of one of the princes of the Church dismissing his own Pontiff's appeal for peace. By October, Bourne must have realised that his own statements had been so unequivocal in opposition to an early peace that he sought to revise his position somewhat. In his Sunday sermon on 14 October, he expressed sorrow on behalf of Catholics at the hostile newspaper coverage of the Peace Note.[42] But by then, it was too late. In any case, even if Bourne had readjusted his observations upon the Peace Note, his true convictions had been found to be on the side of nationalism rather than on the side of Benedict XV and a negotiated end to the war.

Tragic as this might seem, the tragedy was compounded by the fact that Bourne's was not an isolated case. The difference in outlook between the hierarchy and Benedict is further underlined by the fact that the great majority of bishops simply ignored Benedict's Note; an exhaustive search of their pastoral letters around that time does not reveal a single instance where the Note was mentioned. This astonishing silence is eloquent testimony to the sharp disharmonies that war could create, even in communities of faith, and even among those prelates supposedly united by indissoluble bonds of loyalty to Pope and universal Church.

Be that as it may, the first official government reply to the Peace Note came on 28 August 1917 from Woodrow Wilson, the President of the United States. It is not within the scope of this paper to go into great detail in explaining Wilson's reply or the various governments' reactions to it. This diplomatic history has been covered in numerous other studies.[43] Suffice it to say that in his reply, the President peremptorily rejected the Pope's Note, stating that negotiations with Germany, such as the Pope envisaged, were not possible because the current German government was utterly untrustworthy. The British Foreign Office welcomed Wilson's wholly negative and unilateral reply as a way of extricating itself from the potential predicament in which it had found itself upon receiving the Pope's Peace Note. On August 30, the Foreign Office, with evident relief, informed its diplomatic representatives abroad that in view of Wilson's response, the government did not consider it necessary to reply to the Peace Note. As will be seen, this was an unwise move on the part of the government because, although it solved one problem for the Foreign Office, it gave rise to another.

Wilson's reply was received with mixed reaction by the British Catholic leadership. On the whole, the pro-war Catholic press was sympathetic, notwithstanding Wilson's rejection of the Pope's ideas. Most newspapers applauded Wilson's firmness and resolve not to negotiate with the German militarist leadership. *The Tablet* announced its full agreement with Wilson's letter. It empathised with Wilson's perception of the "difficulty of negotiating with a government which regards all treaties as scraps of paper which may be destroyed at will."[44] The *Glasgow Observer*, while not willing to endorse Wilson's reply uncritically, nevertheless expressed gratitude at the "dignified amity and deference" of it.[45] The *Catholic Times*, in comparison, accepted it unreservedly, proclaiming that "the elected representative of... the people of the freest and greatest self-governing nation on earth" was saying that he would have nothing to do with current German leaders.[46]

Other leading Catholics tended to accept Wilson's reply with some reservation. Hugh Edmund Ford, for instance, distinguished between the conflicting duties of Benedict and Wilson. Whereas Wilson, through his letter, sought to uproot the ruthless German autocracy and substitute it with a democratic government, the Pope was the guardian of Christian truth and morals. He was concerned only that governments should be just, honest, and Christian, regardless of whether they were democratic, autocratic, monarchical or republican.[47]

Wilson's reply was not the only reason – it was not even the chief reason – that Benedict's peace effort of August 1917 failed. In analysing the reasons for the failure of Benedict's peace initiative, one must consider a number of factors that combined to render the Peace Note unappealing to the belligerents, chief among them is the notorious article 15 in the secret Treaty of London,[48] signed by Great Britain, France, Russia and Italy in April 1915, when the Allies negotiated with Italy to join the war on their side. The treaty became publicly known after the Bolshevik revolution of early November 1917 in Russia. Soon, the new Russian regime started publishing the secret documents of the Russian Foreign Office, among which was the Treaty of London. These were printed in the *Manchester Guardian*, beginning in mid-December 1917. Article 15 of the treaty stated:

France, Great Britain, and Russia shall support such opposition as Italy may make to any proposal in the direction of introducing a representative of the Holy See in any peace negotiations or negotiations for the settlement of questions raised by the war.[49]

When it became public knowledge in December 1917, article 15 disgusted many people, including non-Catholics. It underlined the apparent hypocrisy of the Entente, which lectured the Pope about appropriate means of ending the war while at the same time plotting to deny him any voice in the peace conference.

As soon as the secret treaty became known, a flurry of diplomatic effort was undertaken by the Foreign Office which lasted well into 1918 in order to defuse – or at least limit – the potentially humiliating situation. The Vatican demanded the complete removal of article 15 from the Treaty of London. On 11 January 1918, Cardinal Gasparri addressed a letter to the British government in which he asserted that the Holy See had received many protests from the Catholic episcopate throughout the world regarding the infamous clause and that he hoped the British Government would eliminate the offensive article.[50] In this way, Gasparri had indirectly warned the British government that if the offensive article was not revoked, strong Catholic pressure from around the globe, including Britain, would be brought against the government to rescind the clause.

The revelation of article 15 hit British Catholics like a thunderbolt from the clear blue sky. They would never have expected their government to repay them for their unwavering and constant loyalty in this way. As soon as Cardinal Bourne learnt of article 15 in December 1917, he made arrangements to visit the Foreign Office and meet Balfour. The Foreign Secretary, although sympathetic to the Vatican, attempted to defend the government. Offering an explanation that scarcely testified to his powers of creative thinking, Balfour told Bourne that the treaty contained "so many clauses of extreme importance" that article 15 had been accepted "almost without attention or discussion" by Grey.[51] Furthermore, Balfour added that the clause was meant to exclude all neutral states. When the Cardinal pointed out that a precise mention of the Holy See was not justified under that category, Balfour explained that his colleagues had not realised Italy's anti-clerical intentions at the signing of the treaty.[52]

Bourne was not the only leading Catholic who was hurt at this seeming betrayal. The majority of other prominent British Catholics deplored the existence of the clause. On 14 February, John McKean, Irish Catholic member for South Monaghan, declared in the House of Commons that article 15 constituted a blunder of the first magnitude and that it was one of "the most extraordinary clauses ever inserted in a treaty."[53]

The Catholic press was no less vociferous in its denunciation of the contentious clause. Most Catholic newspapers agreed that the article achieved nothing but harm to Britain's cause. The *Catholic Times* urged the government to reconsider its attitude to the pressing problem of article 15, which had created a painful impression in the Vatican and offended Catholics throughout the Empire.[54] While *The Universe* could not agree on whether to call the article a colossal blunder or an outrage,[55] the *Catholic Herald* agreed that it was a "gross insult".[56]

The British government had to contend with strong international representations from Catholic hierarchies also. For in its effort to eliminate the article, the Vatican had enlisted the aid of Catholic prelates throughout the world. Soon, the Foreign Office was inundated with protests from Catholic primates requesting the repudiation of article 15, including telegrams from Michael Kelly, the Archbishop of Sydney, and Cardinal Bégin of Quebec.[57] Of more significance, the British government had to contend with protests from Cardinal Gibbons of the U.S.[58] and Cardinal Mercier of Belgium.[59] The government replied by merely acknowledging the receipts of the protests. By early autumn 1918, it had become evident to the most sanguine of Catholic officials that article 15 would not be revoked.

The wider ramification of the existence of article 15 was to create an exasperating difficulty for the British government in its relations with British Catholics. This was compounded by the government's quite deliberate misleading of the country regarding the Pope's Peace Note. On 18 October 1917, C. P. Trevelyan, the Liberal MP and pacifist, asked in the House of Commons whether the government had officially adopted Wilson's reply to the Peace Note as its own.[60] The reply was that it had not – when it clearly had. By January 1918 it still had not sent its own reply to the Pope.

By February, representations to, and agitation against, the government by prominent Catholics in relation to an official response to the Pope's Peace Note began in earnest. On 14 February, John McKean, the Irish Nationalist MP, pressed his attack against the government in the House of Commons. He insisted that it was unacceptable for the government of a great empire to adopt the reply of President Wilson.[61] Even the conservative *Tablet*, which had rejected the Peace Note, found the government's position totally inadequate and criticised it for telling the Pope that it would give his Note "the closest and most serious considerations," and then not replying at all.[62]

The Pope's Peace Note was a lost opportunity to conclude a negotiated peace in August 1917, more than twelve months before World War I ended. The Western Powers were determined to end the war through total victory and as a result Britain refused even to respond to the Peace Note. In their eagerness to present a loyal front to their government, most British Catholics considered the Peace Note an inconvenience. However, once they realized that they were duped by the British government, Catholics throughout the Empire, and British Catholics especially, put the government under immense pressure to reply to the Peace Note and revoke article 15 of the Treaty of London. But this produced no positive results. To British Catholics, this would have seemed to be a bitter blow from the government, who had received their full loyalty and co-operation.

**Notes**

1  J F Pollard, *The Unknown Pope: Benedict XV (1914-1922) and the Pursuit of Peace*, (London: Geoffrey Chapman, 1999).
2  Quoted in A Rhodes, *The Power of Rome in the Twentieth Century: The Vatican in the Age of Liberal Democracies, 1870-1922*, (London: Sidgwick & Jackson, 1983), p. 227.
3  For the full text of the encyclical, see *The Pope and the People: Select Letters and Addresses on Social Questions*, (London: Catholic Truth Society, 1932), pp. 202-217.
4  D R Zivojinovic, *The United States and the Vatican Policies, 1914-1918*, (Colorado: Colorado Associated University Press, 1978), p. 26.
5  Quoted in W H Peters, *The Life of Benedict XV*, (Milwaukee: Bruce Publishing Company, 1959), p. 119.
6  A copy of the letter to the hierarchy is found in Archbishop Whiteside's Letter to the Clergy, 29 Jan. 1915, S1, VII, C/2, Whiteside Papers, Archdiocesan Archives of Liverpool. A complete copy of the Pope's prayer for peace is contained in W. H. Peters, op. cit., p. 123.
7  H E G Rope, *Benedict XV: The Pope of Peace*, (London: John Gifford, 1941), p. 68.
8  *Catholic Times*, 11 Dec. 1914, p. 3.
9  W A S Hewins, a Catholic MP in the House of Commons, for example, recorded in his diary that questions were raised among British Catholics as to the propriety of the Pope's prayer for peace. Hewins Diaries, 4 Feb. 1915, W A S Hewins Papers, Sheffield University Library, Special Collections.
10  *The Tablet*, 17 Apr. 1915, p. 493.
11  *Catholic Times*, 7 May 1915, p. 7.
12  S F Smith, "The Pope's First Encyclical", *The Month*, 125, (Jan. 1915): 1-9.
13  H E G Rope, op. cit., p. 71. The phrase was used by Benedict XV in his allocution to the Sacred College on Christmas Eve, 1914.
14  Ibid. See pp. 88-90. A full translation of the Exhortation was given in *The Tablet*, 7 Aug. 1915, p. 177.

15   H W Flannery (ed.), *Pattern for Peace: Catholic Statements on International Order*, (Westminster: The Newman Press 1962), p. 9.
16   The *Catholic Times* stressed that "The battle is one for liberty, for justice, for humanity. Not one of the Allied Powers dreams of laying down the sword till it has done its work." *Catholic Times*, 13 Aug. 1915, p. 3.
17   *The Universe* asked: "who can say with truth that peace would not be a greater curse to the world than war?" *The Universe*, 20 Aug. 1915, p. 1.
18   For example, W A S Hewins wrote to Cardinal Francis Gasquet, the other British Cardinal, that the only danger to an ultimate British victory was to conclude a false and premature peace. Hewins to Cardinal Gasquet, 15 Oct. 1915, File 875, Cardinal Gasquet Papers, Downside Abbey Archives.
19   There were numerous pastorals and sermons in which the hierarchy expressed their belief in the necessity of the destruction of Prussian militarism, and adjured their flocks to pray for final victory. For a few examples, see Archbishop Whiteside's Report of the Ecclesiastical Education Fund, 8 Mar. 1916, Liverpolitana V, 1915-1919, Whiteside Papers; Sermon of Bishop of Clifton, [July 1916], envelope marked "Personal Envelope", Brindle Papers, Diocesan Archives of Nottingham; Cardinal Francis Bourne's Pastoral of 10 September 1916, reprinted in *The Universe*, 15 Sep. 1916, p. 5. Bourne wrote that ultimate victory depended on God alone and that providence protected the Allies when the enemy ought to have been victorious. See also Bishop Dunn's A Pastoral Letter, Oct. 1916, *(Ad Clerums)*, v.1, 1916-1918/27, Dunn Papers, Diocesan Archives of Nottingham, in which he declared that "Victory will be ours".
20   For a full account of the Guild of the Pope's Peace, see Y Taouk, "The Guild of the Pope's Peace: A British Peace Movement in the First World War", *Recusant History*, 29(2), (October 2008), 252-271.
21   Quoted from the Pope's Exhortation of July 28 in the Preliminary Notice of the Guild of the Pope's Peace, [April 1916], Box XXIV, P IV, Morison Papers, Cambridge University Library, Manuscripts Department. See also H E G Rope, op. cit., p. 89.
22   Bourne to the Duke of Norfolk, 18 Apr. 1916, Box: Nov. 1915-June 1916, Folder: April 1916, 15th Duke of Norfolk Papers, Arundel Castle Archives, Arundel.
23   For the opposition of the Catholic hierarchy and Catholic press to the Guild, see Y Taouk, op. cit.
24   Philip Scheidemann, leader of the Social Democratic Party, and Matthias Erzberger, a leading member of the Catholic Centre Party, instigated the Peace Resolution. They warned the German government that it would be fomenting revolution if it insisted on a war of conquest while the Allies renounced annexations. Chapter 8 of K Epstein's *Matthias Erzberger and the Dilemma of German Democracy*, (Princeton, New Jersey: Princeton University Press, 1959) covers the background and passing of the Peace Resolution in detail.
25   The Pope's Peace Note is analysed point by point in D A Maclean, *The Permanent Peace Program of Pope Benedict XV*, (New York City: Catholic Association for International Peace, 1931). On handing the Peace Note to Count de Salis, the head of the British Mission to the Vatican, on 9 August, Cardinal Gasparri explained that "Although the belligerents were still far apart, recent declarations had brought their

points of view nearer together." The Reichstag had passed a peace resolution while statesmen in England alluded to reparation instead of annihilation. The Pope's aim, explained Gasparri, was to see if recent utterances could initiate an agreement. Confidential Report on Mission to the Holy See, de Salis to Lord Curzon, 25 Oct. 1922, F.O. 371/7671/103, Central Italy (Political), Public Record Office (P.R.O.), London. Thus, in Benedict's view, that was the most propitious moment to launch a peace offensive.

26  See *Peace Action of Pope Benedict XV*, (Washington: Catholic Association for International Peace, [1936]), p. 13.
27  A Rhodes, op. cit., pp. 241-242.
28  See minutes for 10 and 14 Aug. 1917, F.O. 371/3083/216, 225, P.R.O.
29  Balfour to Count de Salis, 21 Aug. 1917, F.O. 371/3083/ 299, P.R.O.
30  For one such example, see "The Vatican and the Germanic Powers", *Contemporary Review*, 112, (Oct. 1917): 403-412. The anonymous author charged that the Note was not only premature, but it was partial to the Central Powers and it reflected the "Teutonic atmosphere" of the Vatican (p. 405).
31  Quoted in A Marrin, *The Last Crusade: The Church of England in the First World War*, (North Carolina: Duke University Press, 1974), p. 227.
32  *The Times*, 16 Aug. 1917, p. 7. *The Times* denounced the epithet in the Peace Note that the war had come to be "more and more a useless massacre". It asserted that because the Allies were fighting for the moral force of right, "the war does not appear to them to be 'more and more a useless massacre,' as the Note describes it".
33  *The Tablet*, 18 Aug. 1917, p. 196.
34  *Glasgow Observer*, 15 Sep. 1917, p. 6.
35  Ibid., 18 Aug. 1917, p. 6.
36  *Catholic Times*, 24 Aug. 1917, p. 3.
37  *Catholic Herald*, 18 Aug. 1917, p. 4.
38  C C Martindale, *Charles Dominic Plater S.J.*, (London: The Ambrose Press, 1922), p. 183.
39  C C Martindale, *The Pope's Peace Note*, (London: Catholic Social Guild, 1917), p. 7.
40  Quoted in A Rhodes, op. cit., p. 242.
41  "The Popes and Peace" (p. 3), [Nov. 1917], Box XXIV, P IV, Morison Papers.
42  *The Tablet*, 20 Oct. 1917, p. 511.
43  A few of the studies include: J L Snell, "Benedict XV, Wilson, Michaelis, and German Socialism", *Catholic Historical Review*, 37(1), (Apr. 1951): 151-178; C Seymour, *The Intimate Papers of Colonel House*, 4 vols., (London: Ernest Benn, 1926-1928), III, chapter 6; C Seymour, *American Diplomacy during the World War*, (Baltimore: The Johns Hopkins Press, 1934), pp. 274-277; T J Knock, *To End all Wars: Woodrow Wilson and the Quest for a New World*, (New York: Oxford University Press, 1992), pp. 139-140. Knock erroneously states that Benedict XV sympathised with the Central Powers. For a critical American view of the Peace Note in 1917, see D Zivojinovic, "Robert Lansing's Comments on the Pontifical Peace Note of August 1, 1917", *Journal of American History*, 56(3), (Dec. 1969): 556-571.
44  *The Tablet*, 1 Sep. 1917, p. 264.

45 *Glasgow Observer*, 1 Sep. 1917, p. 6.
46 *Catholic Times*, 7 Sep. 1917, p. 3.
47 H E Ford, *Pope Benedict's Note to the Belligerents*, (Bristol: J W Arrowsmith, [1917]), p. 12.
48 See, for example, J K Cartwright, "Contributions of the Papacy to International Peace", *Catholic Historical Review*, 8(1), (Apr. 1928), p. 166.
49 W H Peters, op. cit., p. 169. The article was inserted by Italy to prevent the Vatican from attending the future peace conference and raising the unresolved Roman Question.
50 Gasparri to [Lloyd George], 11 Jan. 1918, F.O. 371/3438/16, P.R.O.
51 Quoted in E Oldmeadow, *Francis Cardinal Bourne*, 2 vols., (London: Burns Oates & Washbourne, 1940, 1944), II, p. 114.
52 Ibid.
53 House of Commons Debates, vol. 103, cols., 377, 386. The *Catholic Times* of 22 February 1918 approved of McKean's speech and urged other Catholic members of the House of Commons to support him. The *Catholic Times* commented: "it surely is the duty of Catholic representatives of the people to show that they disapprove of a policy plainly designed to restrict and reduce the influence of the Holy Father" (p. 3).
54 *Catholic Times*, 15 Feb. 1918, p. 3.
55 *The Universe*, 22 Feb. 1918, p. 1.
56 *Catholic Herald*, 23 Feb. 1918, p. 5.
57 See telegrams from Archbishop of Sydney to Balfour, 30 May 1918, F.O. 371/3438/122 and Cardinal Bégin to Balfour, 14 June 1918, F.O. 371/3438/125, P.R.O.
58 J T Ellis, *The Life of James Cardinal Gibbons*, 2 vols., (Milwaukee: The Bruce Publishing Company, 1952), II, p. 270.
59 Cardinal Mercier to Balfour, 2 June 1918, F.O. 371/3438/138, P.R.O.
60 *House of Commons Debates*, vol. 98, col. 246.
61 *House of Commons Debates*, vol. 103, cols. 377-378. The British government never formally endorsed Wilson's reply.
62 *The Tablet*, 23 Feb. 1918, p. 236.

# LINDA KEARNS AND KATHLEEN BARRY IRISH REPUBLICAN FUNDRAISING TOUR, 1924-25

## Anne-Maree Whitaker*

Over a period of five decades from 1880 a number of Irish political activists conducted speaking tours of Australia with the twin aims of imparting information about current political conditions and campaigns, and raising funds. The first such tour following the Easter Rising and resulting War of Independence and Civil War occurred in 1923, when Father Michael O'Flanagan and John Joseph O'Kelly spent five months in Australia before being arrested and deported.[1] The following year a far more successful tour occurred when Linda Kearns and Kathleen Barry arrived in November 1924 and spoke extensively in Victoria, New South Wales and Queensland before their departure in March 1925. Perhaps because their visit was more successful and relatively uncontroversial, it has received little scholarly attention; Patrick O'Farrell devoted three lengthy paragraphs to the 1923 'Envoys' but dismissed the Kearns-Barry visit in a couple of lines.[2]

Both women had impeccable Republican credentials as activists, organisers and speakers. Linda Kearns (later MacWhinney) was a trained nurse who set up a casualty station during the Easter Rising to care for injured Volunteers. She later ran a nursing home while continuing her IRA activity. Kearns was arrested in November 1920 and beaten

*Kathleen Barry and Linda Kearns during their Australian tour.* [Private collection, courtesy Proinnsios Ó Duigneáin]

during interrogation. She was sentenced to 10 years imprisonment for possessing weapons and moved to Liverpool, England. She went on hunger strike demanding to serve her sentence in Ireland, and following her return to Mountjoy prison in Dublin she escaped in October 1921. Together with

---

* Anne-Maree Whitaker is a professional historian with a special interest in Australia's Irish and Catholic history. She was a Councillor of the ACHS from 1995 to 2005.

Kathleen Barry and Mary MacSwiney she remained in the Hammam Hotel in O'Connell Street, Dublin, during the week-long siege that ended in the death of Cathal Brugha during the Civil War in 1922.[3]

Kathleen Barry (later Moloney) was the sister of Kevin Barry, who in November 1920 became the first IRA member executed by the British since 1916. His death made headlines around the world, and the *Catholic Press* in Sydney, under the headline 'War Against Boys', opined: 'Since the days of Judge Jeffreys, and the infamous Norbury, whose name carries the immortal sting of Emmet's dying invective, no judicial crime has paralleled the hanging of Kevin Barry, a medical student, 18 years of age'.[4] Kathleen had a strong Republican record in her own right, fighting on the anti-Treaty side in the Civil War. She went on a speaking tour of the United States in May 1922 and in December 1922 she was asked to reorganise the Irish Republican Prisoners Dependents Fund and acted as general secretary of the fund until September 1924. She was then asked to travel to Australia with Linda Kearns on behalf of the Reconstruction Committee of the IRPDF to raise desperately needed funds to provide financial aid to released prisoners.[5]

The arrival of Kearns and Barry in Melbourne was announced in November 1924 by the *Advocate* newspaper in Melbourne, which stated that Archbishop Daniel Mannix had agreed to act as trustee for donations.[6] The Archbishop chaired their first public meeting, held in the Cathedral Hall, and over the next few weeks they attended various functions around Melbourne.[7] In late December Barry went to Queensland while Kearns remained in Melbourne. Travelling to Brisbane via Warwick and Toowoomba, Barry was accorded a public meeting in the Exhibition Hall chaired by Archbishop James Duhig.[8] In late January she was joined in Queensland by Kearns, and the two women embarked on a punishing itinerary with Barry scheduled to speak in Rockhampton, Mt. Morgan, Mackay, Townsville, Innisfail and Cairns while Kearns travelled to Beaudesert, Ipswich, Warwick, Toowoomba, Maryborough, Bundaberg and Gympie.[9] The women were given an 'all lines' railway pass by the Queensland Railway authorities, and received donations to the Irish Distress Fund from the Premier ('Red Ted' Theodore), the Minister for Lands (William McCormack), Attorney-General (Dublin-born John Mullan), and Mick Kirwin (Assistant Home Secretary).[10]

From Brisbane the two women travelled to Sydney, where on 16 February they held a public meeting at Sydney Town Hall, chaired by Irish-born Coadjutor Archbishop Michael Sheehan. The *Daily Standard* commented:

'Special shorthand experts, thought to be attached to the Police Department, were sent along to the meeting by orders of the Government'.[11] The same day the Sydney Lord Mayor, Paddy Stokes, accorded Kearns and Barry a civic reception.[12] The women spoke at other events around Sydney before splitting up again, with Kearns heading for Queensland to pick up some of the venues which Barry had missed due to flooding, while Barry returned to Victoria for engagements in country towns.[13]

Linda Kearns later said that the tour was difficult at first because of disillusionment caused by the Treaty and Civil War, so that 'the first business of the mission was in a word, spadework'. However the support of the Catholic hierarchy and Catholic newspapers was vital, as 'without them we should have had terrible difficulties'. The fundraising side of the tour was regarded as a great success with around £8000 raised.[14] More importantly, Kearns and Barry avoided conflict with the Catholic hierarchy, unlike O'Flanagan and O'Kelly the year before.[15] Only the Bishop of Rockhampton, Joseph Shiel, refused to support Kearns and Barry's tour on the grounds that it was 'not, as represented, an Irish appeal, but a Republican one'.[16] Their congenial reception also helped to easily deflect an isolated call for their deportation by Charles Oakes, the Nationalist Chief Secretary of New South Wales. Prime Minister Stanley Bruce commented that: 'so far, no action was contemplated by the Commonwealth authorities'.[17] In the end Kearns and Barry left under their own steam in early March 1925.

**Notes**

1 Mark Finnane, 'Deporting the Irish Envoys: Domestic and national security in 1920s Australia', *Journal of Imperial and Commonwealth History*, vol. 41, no. 3, 2013, pp. 403-25.
2 Patrick O'Farrell, *The Irish in Australia*, Sydney: UNSW Press, 1986, pp.291-3.
3 Liz Gillis, *Women of the Irish Revolution*, Cork: Mercier Press, 2014, pp. 143, 208; *Catholic Press* (Sydney), 12 February 1925, p. 19.
4 *Catholic Press* (Sydney), 4 November 1920, p. 27.
5 Papers of Kathleen Barry Moloney, P94, University College Dublin Archives, 'Descriptive Catalogue', iv-v, http://www.ucd.ie/t4cms/p0094-moloney-kathleen-barry-descriptive-catalogue.pdf, viewed 3 March 2016.
6 *Advocate* (Melbourne), 6 November 1924, pp. 20-1.
7 *Advocate* (Melbourne), 20 November 1924, pp. 14, 21.
8 *Telegraph* (Brisbane), 17 January 1924, p. 15.
9 *Catholic Press* (Sydney), 29 January 1925, p. 29.
10 *Advocate* (Melbourne), 12 February 1925, p. 10.

11 *Daily Standard* (Brisbane), 17 February 1925, p. 10; see also *Catholic Press* (Sydney), 12 February 1925, p. 19; *Sydney Morning Herald*, 17 February 1925, p. *9; Freeman's Journal* (Sydney), 19 February 1925, p. 22.
12 *Evening News* (Sydney), 16 February 1925, p. 6.
13 *Advocate* (Melbourne), 19 February 1925, p. 25; *Morning Bulletin* (Rockhampton), 5 March 1925, p. 7 and 12 March 1925, p. 7; *Longreach Leader*, 13 March 1925, p. 24.
14 Proinnsíos Ó Duigneáin, Linda Kearns: *A Revolutionary Irish Woman*, Manorhamilton, Co Leitrim: Drumlin Publications, 2002, pp. 90-97. Quotes from p. 97.
15 Finnane, 'Deporting the Irish Envoys', pp. 410-11.
16 *Catholic Press* (Sydney), 19 March 1925, p. 19.
17 *Maitland Weekly Mercury*, 28 February 1925, p. 3.

# Psychology's Beginnings in Australia and some Early Catholic Responses

## Wanda Skowronksa*

Psychology, as an academic discipline, started relatively late in Australia, when compared with its pioneering beginnings in Europe. The first psychological laboratory, marking the start of 'modern' psychology, was established in 1879 by Wilhelm Wundt at Leipzig University. There were some psychology courses for the benefit of medical students from 1890 onwards at Melbourne university, which had included abnormal psychology courses, as it was then understood. A psychology laboratory was established in Melbourne in 1903 by Dr John Smyth, the Principal of the Teachers' College. Smyth had also been a student at Jena and was impressed by the possibilities of experimental psychology in the training of teachers after visiting Wundt's laboratory in Leipzig, something nearly every student of psychology did in the latter decades of the nineteenth century.

The evident acceptance of 'modern' psychology in Europe, as a study totally compatible with Catholicism, in its *early* phase (1870-1900), was facilitated by the fact that many Catholics studied at Wundt's laboratory – for example the renowned American Thomist, Father Aloysius Pace (who set up the first psychology department in an American university), Armand Thierry from France who set up the first French laboratory under the guidance of Cardinal Mercier), and myriad other Catholic psychologists such as Kazimierz Twardowski, Johannes Lindworsky, Albert Michotte and Agostino Gemelli among many others. There would have been no dispute about the definition of the 'person' under study being embedded in a very long Judeo-Christian philosophical and theological legacy, informing an understanding of psychology as much as nineteenth century science did. Cardinal Mercier was adamant that psychology was a valid field of inquiry, and need not be opposed to the of metaphysics and the theological anthropology of Aristotle and St Thomas. His work *Psychologie, Les Origines de la Psychologie Contemporaine* (1892), a compilation of lectures given to his students at Louvain, expressed his view that psychology based on a sound metaphysics should be open to all scientific development.[1]

* Wanda Skowronska is a Catholic psychologist and author living and working mainly in Sydney. She is a regular contributor to the Australian Catholic journal *Annals Australasia*. Her book *Catholic Converts from Down Under ... And All Over* was reviewed in the 2015 *JACHS*. She earned her PhD at the John Paul II Institute in Melbourne in 2011 where she does some sessional lecturing.

By the time Australians had jumped on the psychology bandwagon, the influences of Freud and the behaviourists were establishing ever more strongly the new psychological Zeitgeist and becoming increasingly entrenched in the era's deterministic and materialist views. These influences assumed very different ideas of the person and the ends of life from those a Catholic would assume – that the human person reflects the *Imago Dei,* the Trinity, and was made to share eternal life with God. No Catholic university as yet existed in Australia – along the lines of Catholic University of America which was established in 1887 and which established its first psychology department in 1890, nor like Louvain where the first psychological laboratory was set up in 1891 – where students integrated Catholic philosophical and theological anthropology alongside experimental psychology without any ideological pressure. One might ask why it would be important to examine the assumptions of the human person in experimentally based areas of psychology? While there are many evidence-based fields of psychology – forensic psychology, psycholinguistics, cognitive psychology, neuropsychology and psychometrics to name a few – it is counselling psychology that was less evidence-based from the start (though not now) and prone to anti-metaphysical agendas being promoted through its altered and often hidden philosophical assumptions. And counselling psychology was a great preoccupation of psychology, under whose banner many people sought help, as Phillip Reiff stated half a century ago, in his account *The Triumph of the Therapeutic* (1966). And one could ask simply – if one does not understand what a person is, then who is one trying to help? It is not only counselling psychology, but any field of psychology that is based on a philosophical anthropology of some kind.

A survey of some of the early psychology appointments in Australia does not yield any evidence of adherence to the traditional Judeo-Christian philosophical anthropology, though it might to some extent still be assumed as cultural capital. Ronald Taft points to two intellectual streams that influenced this early phase of Australian psychology.[2] First, the strong empirical orientation of British philosophy – particularly that of John Stuart Mill and Alexander Bain who 'attempted to develop a systematic theory of psychology built on complex thought, attention, and constructive cognition.' A second intellectual influence was to be found in such thinkers as Darwin, Spencer, Galton and, later, McDougall. Taft observes: 'This influence manifested itself in an interest in instinct, abilities and adaptation to the demands of life, and its effects were to be found in medical schools as well as philosophy departments.'[3]

The first Australian appointments in psychology indicate wider European influence, though they occurred after the initial decades of Catholic and Protestant crowding of Wundt's laboratories. The first professor of psychology in Australia was Tasman Lovell (1878 - 1958) who became McCaughey associate professor of psychology at the University of Sydney in 1921 becoming full professor in 1928.[4] W M O'Neil notes that Lovell was well read in Wundtian experimental psychology, in Binet's contributions to mental measurement.[5] saying that ... 'it was largely through his [Lovell's] efforts that Fisher Library in the University of Sydney has such a splendid collection of early French and German psychological material.[6] Other early appointments include that of H L Fowler as Associate Professor in the University of Western Australia; Bernard Muscio, Challis Professor of Philosophy 1922-6, whose published pioneering lectures on Industrial Psychology (1917), sought the practical application of 'the science of psychology' not only to industry, but also to Education, medicine and law; Stanley Porteous, who worked with disabled children from 1913 onwards; and devisor of the Porteous Maze test; Gilbert Phillips who ran experimental psychology classes at Sydney Teachers' College.[7]

While it is difficult to find any written reflection and participation in psychology by Catholic academics in the early decades of the twentieth century, there arose at that time, some robust commentary and questioning of psychology in non-academic Catholic media sources. It principally takes the form of a critique of Freud – with whom Australian academic psychology would have been well acquainted by now - and although it comes from 'non psychological' sources, it encapsulates in many ways the ideas that were to come from future later critiques of Freud, which did come from more academic and psychological sources. For example, an unsigned review of a book by Rudolf Allers in the *Catholic Weekly* in 1947, makes very clear that Allers, a psychotherapist and well-educated in Thomism, disagreed with Freud's worldview, and had some pertinent things to say to Catholics in Australia and the reviewer gives a favourable evaluation of Allers' book, *Difficulties in Life* (1939).[8] He notes that Allers speaks from his position a professor at the Catholic University of America in seeing Freudian psychotherapy as totally incompatible with Catholicism.[9] Allers was a Catholic psychologist and philosopher who studied with Freud in Vienna - and who left the Freudian circle, after deep disputes with Freud's overemphasis on the sexual instinct as the basis of human behaviour and his anti-religious stance. The reviewer makes the point that before pursuing any psychotherapy uncritically, whether as a student or a person needing help, a Catholic, like Allers, needs to ask what philosophical principles undergird any psychotherapeutic approach - for they might lead to beliefs which contradict a person's moral code. For example, pointing to Freudian psychotherapy, there could be no agreement from a Catholic with its view that 'denied sin and would supplant confession'.[10] In this simple statement is encapsulated much of the Freudian assault on objective morality and on the belief that a psychotherapist alone can liberate a person from inner distress, sidelining the value of a spiritual dimension in healing and usurping the role of the priest as a spiritual guide. The reviewer states that Allers' championed the traditional Catholic view that in 'getting to know oneself, the greatest thinkers of the ages have long held that the advice of a 'director' is indispensable'.[11] He acknowledges the concomitant need for psychology in dealing with deep-seated 'mental barriers' - and this in an era before the first Diagnostic and Statistical Manual of Mental Disorders (DSM1) had appeared and before the first antipsychotic medications became available for serious illnesses such as schizophrenia.[12] The Australian reviewer goes on the describe Allers' classification of personality types, again prescient, in an era where any such classification was in its infancy. The reviewer also makes reference to other books by Allers. The latter wrote several works critiquing Freudian psychotherapy, the most outstanding among them arguably being, *The Successful Error: A Critical Study Of Freudian Psychoanalysis* (1940).[13]

Alongside this Australian philosophical critique were the views of those who either were naively in awe of the new field, or tended to view all psychology as harmless. Such views were also expressed in the Catholic media. For instance, a Fr Dalton is recorded as saying, in a public talk in 1948:

> The high-sounding 'complexes' of the psychologist's text-book are, for the most part, only variations on the theme of the seven capital sins which our children recite from the catechism.[14]

It is interesting that the Australian reviewer of Allers' work – quoted earlier – says exactly the opposite – that Freud's worldview is opposed to the Catholic view of sin, and complexes cannot be equated to sin. In fact, Allers' negative assessment of much of Freud's thought is echoed in the later critique penned by Freud's ally and friend Erich Fromm, not a Christian, who was to question his colleague's worldview in *The Greatness and Limitations of Freud's Thought* (1979). Fromm especially questioned the underlying assumption of the Oedipus Complex driving all human behaviour, saying Freud grossly misread the Greek myth from which it is taken, which in fact sees incest as horrifying and exceptional and to be punished by the gods. Incest was objectively wrong for the Greeks, certainly not an acceptable explanation for ordinary family life.[15] So even a non Christian like Fromm can see that Freud's categorisations of good and bad behaviour have nothing to do with the Greek worldview from which he took his template for family life – a question of marked inaccuracy, as much as of moral misreading of the Oedipus Myth. There were many critiques of Freud yet to come but the point is here, that the Australian reviewer of Allers' superbly written academic critiques (not well known nowadays) promulgated the latter's views in the mainstream Catholic media and were available to a wide audience.

Another source of similarly insightful Australian commentary on psychology came from none other than Dr Rumble's one-hour 'Question Box' program which began in 1928 and was aired on Sydney's 2SM radio station, and was heard all over Australia and New Zealand. For five years Fr (Dr) Rumble answered questions on every subject and gave particularly intelligent commentary and critique as regards psychology - in fact not long after the first psychology department was formed at the University of Sydney. The longest discourses on psychology can be read in Volume 3 of *Radio Replies* (1979, 1942) which is the published version of his answers.[16] From question 1079–1094, he gives clear accounts in a very synthesised form, of what he called ' 'New Psychology' and ' Psychoanalysis'.

For example in reply to a question as to whether psychology was a science (there were boundary issues from the outset of modern psychology), Dr Rumble answers:

> Yes within its proper sphere. Its duty is to observe arrange, and classify facts making allowance for all the facts of human personality, including free will but psychology does not mean determinism. ....It is unscientific to deny free will and philosophical nonsense.[17]

Continuing this discussion of the problems of classification and philosophical assumptions of psychology, Dr Rumble explains:

> One division of experimental psychology is called medical psychology and its method is called psycho-therapy, or the healing of the mind of the patient by the mind of the practitioner. ... No one can doubt the connection between mental states and certain psychical and moral disorders.[18]

Here he is pointing out that not only psychical disorders but moral disorders can be assisted by psychology – a very prophetic view of the future cooperation between clergy and psychologists in dealing with addictions, abortion grief and various personality disorders. While going on to say, 'psycho-therapy has wrought many cures. ... not due to magic or any superstitious elements ... but due to the use of his own mind and will by the patient under the direction of one capable of inducing in him a completely changed mental outlook', he concludes that while 'No Catholic, therefore, could condemn the practice of psycho-therapy in itself', he would have to be on the lookout for 'abuses in the name of psycho-therapy' and outlines what he means:

> And abuses are certainly present in that form of psycho-therapy which is known as Freudian psycho-analysis.[19]

Specifying one of the most important problems in Freudian psychology as 'determinism' which contradicts the Catholic understanding of free will, Dr Rumble did not throw all psychology to the dogs. In answer to a question as to whether Catholics can study or make use of psychology, there is no blanket condemnation of the field, as was to issue from future critics, particularly from those espousing biblical counselling, but rather a warning that prudence was necessary in evaluating each approach on its merits.

> They may make the fullest possible use of it, provided it remains practical psychology and does not through misinterpretation and misdirection, trespass on the province of religion and morals.[20]

This advocacy of a judicious approach stood in contrast to the thrall in which many Catholics were held with regard to Freud (and perhaps even more so later, with Jung). It also predates similar conclusions by future Catholic psychologists such as Paul Vitz whose seminal work *Psychology as Religion* (1977) started a wave of Catholic critique of the assumptions underlying the various psychological approaches to counselling in the modern and post-modern era. When one adds the philosophical and theological anthropology present throughout the *Radio Replies*, to be clearly articulated by the future Pope John Paul II and taught at the Institutes bearing his name, one is presented with a widely available, clearly reasoned, intelligent and understandable account of the benefits and dangers of 'modern psychology' in its relatively early phase in Australia.

Dr Rumble saw the problems of boundary definition in psychology and the concomitant attempts to lure Catholics away from their rich theological and philosophical legacy. He saw what future historian of psychology, Sigismund Koch observed decades later, that psychology was not an autonomous field, reduced to Comtean positivism, it was not 'a single or coherent discipline but rather a collectivity of studies of varied cast, some few of which may qualify as a science while most do not'.[21] As a recovering behaviourist Koch strongly insisted that the study of psychology necessitated the study of philosophy. One suspects Dr Rumble would have been at ease with Koch's future advocacy for this more multi-faceted approach to the study of psychology – proposing the term 'Psychological Studies' to encapsulate the ambiguity and 'mystery' of the human person.[22] And in the midst of the growing anti-religious Zeitgeist of the early twentieth century, Australian Catholics were fortunate to have access to pertinent and perceptive commentary of a very high order, in their mainstream media, concerning the strengths and weaknesses of psychology's ever burgeoning and enthralling influence.

**Notes**

1   A comprehensive study of the involvement of Catholics in the early phase of modern psychology is: Henryk Misiak and Virginia Staudt, *Catholics in Psychology: A Historical Survey* (NY: McGraw-Hill, 1954).
2   Ronald Taft, 'Psychology and its history in Australia', *Australian Psychologist*, 1982. Volume 17, Issue 1:31 ff.
3   Ibid., 32.
4   More information on Lovell's life and career can be obtained from W M O'Neil, "Teaching and Practice of Psychology in Australia in the First Phases" Ronald Taft and Mary Nixon (Eds.), *Psychology in Australia: Achievements and Prospects* (South Australia: Pergamon Press, 1977), Chapter 1: 2-34.; Ronald Taft 'Psychology and its history in Australia', *Australian Psychologist*, 1982.Volume 17, Issue 1:31-39; W M O'Neil, 'Lovell, Henry Tasman (1878–1958)', *Australian Dictionary of Biography*, National Centre of Biography, Australian National University, http://adb.anu.edu.au/biography/lovell-henry-tasman-7247/text12553, published first in hardcopy 1986, accessed online 1 September 2016; and the following link lists Lovell as a member of the Sydney University Lodge - http://www.lodgeunisyd.org/historyoflodgeuniversityofsydney
5   W M O'Neil, "Teaching and Practice of Psychology in Australia in the First Phases". In. Ronald Taft and Mary Nixon (Eds.), *Psychology in Australia: Achievements and Prospects* (South Australia: Pergamon Press, 1977), 5.
6   Ibid., 5-6.
7   A more detailed account of Australian pioneer psychologists can be found in: W M O'Neil, "Teaching and Practice of Psychology in Australia in the First Phases" Ronald Taft and Mary Nixon (Eds.), *Psychology in Australia: Achievements and Prospects* (South Australia: Pergamon Press, 1977), Chapter 1: 2-34.
8   Unsigned Review, 'Psychology for Catholics', *Catholic Weekly*, Sept 11, 1947, 3.
9   Rudolf Allers, *Self-Improvement* (US: Benzinger Brothers, 1939).
10  Unsigned Review, 'Psychology for Catholics', *Catholic Weekly*, Sept 11, 1947, 3.

11 Ibid.,3..
12 *The Diagnostic and Statistical Manual of Mental Disorders* (DSM1), used by psychiatrists and clinical psychologists to diagnose mental disorders, appeared in its first edition in 1952 and was largely Freudian in content. It is now in its 5th edition which was published in 2015.
13 Rudolf Allers, *The Successful Error; A Critical Study Of Freudian Psychoanalysis* (New York, Sheed & Ward, 1940).
14 Fr Dalton, MSC. 'New Psychology, Old Morality', *Catholic Weekly*, March 25, 1948:4.
15 Erich Fromm, *The Greatness and Limitations of Freud's Thought* (London: Jonathan Cape, 1980, 1979), 37.
16 Fathers Rumble and Carty, *Radio Replies*, (US: Tan Books and Publishers Inc., 1979, originally published in 1942 by *Radio Replies Press*, St Paul, Minnesota), Vol 3, 1084. Henceforth Rumble, *RR - 3*.
17 Rumble, *RR - 3*, Question 1083. Interestingly historian of psychology Sigismund Koch states - in Koch and Leary, *A Century of Psychology as Science* (New York: McGraw-Hill Book Company, 1985: 17-18) that Wilhelm Wundt's view of the nature of psychology as regards the *Naturwissenschaften* (roughly translated as the sciences) and *Geisteswissenschaften* (humanities) changed considerably over time. At first, Wundt, generally seen as the 'founder' of modern psychology, saw the field more as within the *Naturwissenschaften* category but by the time of his *Grundzüge der physiologischen Psychologie* (1873) he saw it as occupying an intermediate position between the *Naturwissenschaften* and *Geisteswissenschaften*. Koch notes that by the time of his later work MetodenLehre (1883), his view was that psychology lay within the *Geisteswissenschaften*.
18 Rumble, *RR - 3, Q. 1085.*
19 Ibid.
20 Rumble, *RR - 3, Q 1086.*
21 Sigmund Koch, 'The Nature and Limits of Psychological Knowledge: Lessons of a Century *qua* "Science"', *American Psychologist*, 36, March, 1981, 268.
22 Sigmund Koch, 'The Nature and Limits of Psychological Knowledge: Lessons of a Century qua Science,' in. *A Century of Psychology as Science*. Eds. Sigmund Koch and David E Leary, McGraw-Hill Book Company, New York, 1985, 93.

## Golden Jubilee of Ordination Homily: We Few, We Happy Few: A Drama in Three Scenes, with a Prologue and Final Apotheosis!

### John de Luca*

For fifty years now I have always, or almost always, spoken without notes, preferring to talk directly to those who had chosen to listen. But on this significant occasion, when we are celebrating the end point (or perhaps more accurately the starting point) of what that band of idealistic young men who assembled at St Columba's College Springwood in 1959 and 1960 saw as a goal worth striving for, I have decided to impose a little more discipline on myself by writing out what I want to say in full, and reading it. To give some structure to my words I have conceived this as an occasional address rather than a more familiar homily, and cast it in dramatic terms. So, appropriately enough in this Shakespearian four-hundredth anniversary year, when all the world's a stage, and we the players on it, I have given it a title: *We Few, We Happy Few: A Drama in Three Scenes*, with Prologue and Final Apotheosis.

### PROLOGUE:

A friend who is a retired Anglican rector told me recently that, when he was training for the ministry, he was instructed never to mention himself when preaching. I'm afraid that is a piece of good advice that I have rarely followed. In fact, when preaching, I quite regularly try to start by mentioning some incident in my own life that could parallel the experiences of my listeners, and so lead into what I want to say. I've never liked laying down the law from on high, as it were. So: spoiler alert! I'm going to speak about three pieces of advice given to me on or about Ordination Day in 1966, in the hope that what was said to me so long ago might possibly strike a resounding chord in your own experience.

### SCENE ONE:

St Mary's Cathedral, Sydney, very cold in mid-winter, and very early in the morning. Ordinations had to be early then, owing to the old laws relating to the Eucharistic fast. Excitement and anticipation tempered the frigid conditions, and, with warm hearts, those who had just been ordained proceeded to give their first priestly blessings. Traditionally, the first blessing was reserved

---

* Rev. Dr John de Luca. Historian, musician and Pastor Emeritus of the Parish of St Mary and St Joseph Maroubra Bay/Beach.

for one's mother, father and family, and only then given to anyone who requested it. Friends and strangers would present themselves for a blessing to those who had just been ordained. An elderly priest, unknown to me, came for a blessing. At least I thought that he was elderly. He was probably younger than we are now, but at age twenty four one's seniors often seemed impossibly old. After receiving his blessing, this priest looked up at me and said earnestly "Look after yourself, son, because no-one else will!" That brought me down to earth a little. I wondered what the future might hold for one embarking on the celibate life. I had had little experience of normal life, having led a cloistered existence for eight years after leaving school. We had been trained in the seminary to be obedient and self-contained, but not much attention had been given to our psychological suitability for the single life. The presumption was that the charism of ordination would be enough to enable us to function without the consolation of a soul-mate or the warmth of human intimacy. Clearly this assumption was, in many cases, not well-based. We had been schooled to distrust emotions, to hold ourselves aloof, to sit in judgment on others. Canon Law accorded special status to priests as sacred persons, an assertion that many of us have come to question over the years. But the thought of being left alone in old age hardly seemed relevant in those heady days. Of course, some of our number were older and more experienced in the ways of the world when entering the seminary. But the majority of us had come straight from school: in my case at age sixteen. Apart from the inculcation of a need for prayer and sacrifice, the only practical advice that I can remember receiving from the rectors at Springwood and Manly on how to cope with the demands of priesthood was Monsignor Charles Dunne telling us that we should become accustomed to reading a good book in the privacy of our room. What's more, Charlie told us that we didn't necessarily have to read that book: just to feel it was often enough! Monsignor James Madden at St Patrick's College, Manly, was even more bizarre, telling us that when we felt frustrated, we should get in our car and go for "a scorch". We knew that he meant "a burn", but Jimmy really wasn't much in touch with the world on which we were about to be unleashed. The only truly practical piece of advice that I can remember him giving was that, if we were called out on a sick call in the middle of the night, to remember to pull up the blankets before we left so that the bed might still have some warmth on our return!

Now, more than half a century later, whenever I may be inclined to mock those mentors of the past, I need only to look at my own incomprehension of the vastly different world we inhabit today: the world of tattoos and facial hair, the world of technology, instant communications, social media, serial marriages and self expression, the world of sometimes murderous religious fundamentalism and intolerance. What we then found odd or amusing in our elders, the same could well be said of us now. Now we are the dinosaurs. The men who tried to mould us in the seminary were many and varied. Some were of impressive intellect, some were "duds", but most, I believe, had our best interests at heart. They had experienced already what we could only dimly perceive, and in their own way tried to prepare us for what lay ahead.

That anonymous priest, who made the heartfelt remark to me on ordination day, knew the score. Perhaps he could have been a little more positive and have advised me that we should look after one another. As a group, I think that our class has tried to do that in some ways. The fact that we have managed to sustain an annual reunion over the last fifty years, and that we take our mutual friendships as a "given' in life, is a sign of that. The business of 'looking out for one another' was forged in seminary days, when we tended to think that the authorities 'had it in for us'. On that score I am reminded of the antinomian attitude of Sebastian Flyte in Evelyn Waugh's book 'Brideshead Revisited'. "Sebastian Contra Mundum" sums it up. Waugh's character (he of the teddy bear and plovers eggs, if you are familiar with the story) felt that he was up against it. Perhaps the world wasn't particularly against us, but we closed ranks, and here, half a century later, our bonds remain strong.

**SCENE TWO:**

The first Monday 'off' after the first week in the first parochial appointment, January 1967, in my case, at St Peter's, Surry Hills. Monday was always 'curates day off'. Before any other activity, I headed for home to spend some time with my parents in Coogee. I would have travelled by bus, since we were not yet allowed to own cars in those days in the Archdiocese of Sydney. My father, then aged fifty two, had been an invalid for the previous four years. He had had his first stroke at age forty eight when we were in First Theology at Manly in 1963. Jimmy Madden called me to his office in the middle of that year to tell me that my father was in Lewisham Hospital. He had crashed his car while driving as a result of that stroke, and was never to work or drive again. Jimmy told me to "pray that the Lord takes him". I of course, would do no such thing. Right through our time at Manly dad was always having minor strokes, going back and forth to hospital with a regularity that we had come to take for granted. Somehow he had retained the strength to see the eldest of his six children ordained and embarked on parochial life. Dad, who had a truck for his business, was always being called on by the priests, brothers and nuns of our parish to carry things for them. His respect for the religious in our community obviously had some influence on my aspiration to the priesthood. He never questioned my wish to go to the seminary, although, years after his death, my mother told me that he had wept all the way home after driving me to Central Station for the reserved carriage that took students to Springwood for the new seminary year in 1959. He had lost his firstborn, the one who was meant to be the doctor of the family! Now, eight years later, on that first Monday home, I found my mother searching for dad. He had wandered off and was nowhere to be found. So I scoured the surrounding streets, eventually finding him in his pyjamas and dressing gown, and led him home. After settling him, I proceeded to deliver him a lecture, telling him that he wasn't to leave the house since it caused distress to mum. Then, in a moment of lucidity, he addressed me quite formally: "Now that you're a priest, remember who you are and where you came from, and don't get too big for your boots!" Stunned, I stormed off in a huff. But those were the last words that my father ever spoke to me. He died suddenly the following Sunday. His was the first funeral I ever performed. His words are seared into my consciousness, and I offer them to you now for your consideration even at this late stage in our own lives. The sentiment may be commonplace, and our circumstances greatly changed, but the validity of my father's admonition remains. If the word 'humility' comes from the Latin 'humus', then we should never forget those who are the source of our earthly being, as the fourth commandment justly reminds us.

**SCENE THREE:**

Somewhat later in life, but still in the early years of priesthood. My mother's eldest brother, Henry William Slattery, (universally known as 'Mick' Slattery) had been ordained in 1932, and was the strongest male influence in the first three formative years of my life since my father was overseas in the Australian army, called away to the Second World War. Mick was an experienced pastor whose advice I valued, especially in the early years of ministry. One gem of wisdom he imparted to me, by way of a caution, was: "Keep away from Bishops: they're vindictive!" Now I'm not suggesting that all bishops are vindictive, or that one should refuse to respect one's bishop. So Mick's remark needs to be put into context. He had certainly witnessed instances where priests had suffered grief at the hands of their Ordinaries.

Mick was ordained when Michael Kelly was Sydney's archbishop, and was a close observer of Norman Gilroy, his first cousin. When Mick, in old age, was asked by Ted Clancy to step down as a parish priest, he did what he was asked. I questioned him on this, remarking that he had tenure, and didn't have to comply. He simply said to me "I've never said no to a bishop, and I'm not going to start now". So the advice to "keep away from bishops" had a deeper meaning. I was being told not to be ambitious for career advancement. It is a truth universally acknowledged that some priests are inclined to "hitch their wagon to a star". Clerical ambition, I was being warned, is the antithesis of what we ought to be concerned about. Respect for legitimate authority is one thing, but sucking-up to the powerful is quite another, and almost always distasteful. Of course, telling bishops what they need to hear, rather than what they might prefer to hear, is not always conducive to advancement. But it is surely the better path.

Looking at our class, I don't believe that any of our number went out of his way get ahead. I remember one of our number once saying to me long ago: "Wouldn't it be great to be a bishop. Think of the good you could do". But I think that that was just a passing fancy, and something that he certainly resiled from in later life. Certainly none of us has had the burden of high office imposed on him, thanks be to God! Those who have left ministry seem to me to have successfully negotiated the greater challenges of life which we who stayed have studiously avoided. So I would like to pay tribute to-day to the sacrifices that our brothers who have returned to the lay state have made over the years, and to thank them for their example and encouragement. Although some might not like the inference, their concern for others seems to me to be manifestly sacerdotal, and a reflection of the formation that has marked us all for life. These days one hears much criticism in certain quarters of the word "ontological" when used to describe the character imposed at ordination to priesthood. I'm no theologian, and I don't intend to buy into that particular debate. But I do believe that our seven or eight years together in the seminary have made us, as a group, people who want to serve, rather than to be served. And that, it seems to me, is something worth celebrating to-day.

And now finally,

**THE APOTHEOSIS:**

I first came across that word 'Apotheosis' when I was twelve years old. My mother, encouraging my obvious interest in classical music, took me to a performance of Tchaikovsky's ballet 'Swan Lake'. The drama concluded with the deaths of the proponents who, in that particular production by the Borovansky Ballet Company, after drowning in the lake, came back to life as swans. As they glided across the lake, the great melody changed from the minor key to the major. If that sounds too technical, think of it as changing from sad to happy. It's a musical trick that always works on our subconscious even if we think that we are not particularly musical. Of course, 'Apotheosis' means turning into a god, or having the gods intrude into the lives of mortals to sort out the messes that we so often get ourselves into. Classical Greek drama often concluded with a 'deus ex machina' solution to life's problems. 'God from a machine' was a reference to the stage machinery, generally some sort of a crane, which lowered a god from above the stage to the world inhabited by humans, bringing resolution to that which was out of kilter. So, like the gods in true dramatic convention, I now seek to resolve some of the issues raised by the three pieces of advice given to me after ordination (from an anonymous priest, from my father, and from my uncle) and to see how they might have some transformative application to us all.

Many of our seminary friends, who have died already, have no further need of resolution. As is our duty, we pray for the repose of their souls, convinced, however, that their good deeds have preceded them, and that they have little need of the prayers that we freely make for them. We who remain all have issues to attend to. Looking after ourselves, physically, mentally and spiritually is a continuing challenge. Remembering where we came from and not getting too big for our boots has not become less important even after the passing of our parents. And tempering ambition, not dwelling on real or imagined slights received in the course of our lives, is something that identifies us with Christ. Did he not warn us when speaking of his own sufferings: "If they have done this in the green wood, what will they do in the dry?"

In typical male fashion, most of us are reticent when it comes to discussing our personal spirituality, so I hope that you won't think ill of me if mention some of the principles that I remember our seminary lecturers stressing at different times, and which have certainly guided me on my journey through this sometime seemingly crazy church where the leadership often seems to be at odds with common sense. George Joiner told us in his very first lecture to us that everything that we would learn about the divine was analogical. If we didn't understand analogy, we would understand nothing. At the tail and of my life I am glad to remember this when I hear those who speak so confidently about the immutability of what are really just their opinions, and often just a reflection of their personal inadequacies. It is all too easy to speak as if one has a direct line to the Almighty! My guiding principles have included Ockham's Razor (*entia non sunt multiplicanda sine necessitate*) which says to look for a natural explanation before invoking the supernatural; St Augustine, for all his faults (remember Martin Luther was an Augustinian, and inclined to pessimism) taught us that "Grace builds on nature"; the Christian Humanism of the Renaissance proclaimed Man, under God, as the Measure of All Things; Canon Law asserted that laws were for people ('leges propter hominess"), and not *vice versa*; Canon Law again taught us that "leges stricte interpretande sunt". Laws are to be interpreted as narrowly as possible so as to allow maximum liberty to the individual; Hegel's Principle of the Dialectic (Thesis: Antithesis: Synthesis), from the first moment I encountered it in the History of Philosophy course, has seemed to me to be a rationally adequate way of analysing the progress of human history, with, of course, the *caveat* of avoiding the pitfalls of Marxist Dialectic Materialism which would almost certainly get one into trouble with the Congregation for the Doctrine of the Faith; then we have "Ecclesia supplet", and *"epikaia"*. For better or for worse, these are the principles that have helped guide me through the labyrinth of human existence, and I suspect that they have, consciously or unconsciously, influenced us all. And they all sprang from our sometimes obscurantist Tridentine seminary education almost a lifetime ago! So it wasn't all bad.

I made a passing reference earlier to Evelyn Waugh's novel 'Brideshead Revisited'. Waugh, a practicing but disappointed Catholic, died on Easter Sunday 1966 fortified (like his creation Lord Marchmain) by the sacraments of Holy Mother Church. Many regard Waugh as the best prose stylist writing in English in the twentieth century, and 'Brideshead Revisited' was one of his most significant achievements. Waugh described the general theme of his creation as "the operation of divine grace on a group of diverse but closely connected characters". That surely perfectly describes us. We are certainly a diverse group of characters, and I have no doubt that divine grace is at work even amongst us! Whether we like it or not, we cannot escape the action of divine grace working through our parents, family, friends, teachers and the people whom we rub-up against each day. Acknowledging what we owe to one another is not so different, I would contend, to what St Paul was 'getting at' two thousand years ago when he pointed to the Athenian altar inscribed "To An Unknown God". Sometimes we fail to recognise what is happening more deeply under the shallow veneer of our daily lives. Perhaps what we are celebrating to-day has greater significance than we might at first be aware of. And so I say 'thank you' to all of you, companions on the journey. You have contributed more to my life than I perhaps have acknowledged in the past, and, perhaps, in my own small way, I may have added a gloss to your story too.

Christian hope in the Resurrection serves the function that apotheosis did in Greek drama. It reflects the desire for transformation. When Jesus sent out the disciples to preach, he told them to tell people that the Kingdom of Heaven was close at hand, indeed that it was among them already. Our friendship, our unity of spirit, betokens the heavenly life, where every tear will be wiped away. That is our hope, and it is my prayer for you.

# A MEMOIR OF THE VALUE OF A RELIGIOUS LIFE FOR ONE INDIVIDUAL

## Moira O'Sullivan RSC*

The short version of this talk is: **God is the true reality in whom and for whom we were made, so any life that keeps God in sight is in touch with reality.**

However, because it's still Lent, we're having the longer version, with

*Front Row: Sisters: Aloysius Murphy, Gabriel Burke, Rev. Mother Francis McGuigan, Mother Xavier Cunningham, Sisters; Gonzaga Russell, Ignatius D'Arcy*

*Second Row: Sisters: Fidelis Hogan, Margaret Ennis, Dominic Poppenhagen, Brendan Lynch, DeSales Cleary, Leonard Armstrong-O'Byrne, Cecilia Bruton, Agnes Shorthill (last surviving member of the Parramatta Community)*

*Third Row: Sisters: Rodriguez Jones, Clement Stapleton, Gertrude Healy, Teresa Lockington, Laurentia Jaguers, Alexis O'Gorman, Fachnan Sheehy, Benedict O'Brien*

December 1895: Sisters at St Vincent's Hospital, Sydney, with the superior general M M Francis McGuigan

* After secondary teaching and theological and biblical study in Rome, Moira lectured in theological colleges and seminaries in Sydney and PNG. She did her PhD on the conflicts faced by Sisters of Charity in Australia, 1838-1859. At present, her main interest is the history of her Congregation.

the warning that often prefaces works of fiction: 'No aspects of this story of religious life are taken from anyone else's experience.' Also, it will not talk of what religious Sisters have done, from fear of being 'celebratory' rather than 'objective'.[1] In case it seems as if my life has been cherrypicked for the good bits, bad times aren't regretted when I look back, because of what they taught.

Each person is different, so the story of each religious life is different. This one is **told to show that religious life is as satisfying and fulfilling as any other**, so please don't discourage your children, grandchildren or friends from taking it on. Like any other life, it has its ups and downs. Everyone's span is rather like the whole sweep of the Old Testament: Here are these hopeless people, always doing the wrong thing and getting into trouble, but God never gives up on them. If that isn't the story of your life, it certainly is of mine.

Radio National has a programme titled, 'The year that made me.' I could choose several, but 1954 stands out. Charles Dickens provides the vocabulary: 'It was the best of times; it was the worst of times.' It was the year I entered the Sisters of Charity. It was the best of times, because the novitiate gave time for prayer, as well as for fun and friendships, and we were taught to meditate. It was the worst of times, because of the anguish of breaking off from family, friends, and my dearly beloved, especially for someone who wanted to have children. About two months ago, a young Catholic mother seriously asked me how I could possibly live without sex. I found out.

Some recent novels, if not total fantasy, introduce something inexplicable. Eleanor Catton's *The Luminaries*[2] has a character who is psychic; and Jessie Burton's *The Miniaturist* features a woman who apparently predicts the future of persons she has not met. Do these show that we realise that this world is not enough? Whatever the answer, it's my rationale for claiming that there is no totally human explanation for religious life, historical or otherwise.

### Anti-Catholic prejudice in the 1950s

Religious life used to be denigrated mainly by those outside the Catholic church but now even believers see it as unnecessary, even unnatural.

Anti-catholic prejudice explained some early opposition. As a young religious, I was spat on two or three times. Some people believed that nuns were imprisoned. Once in the city a woman grabbed my superior's arm, telling me to run for it, that she'd hang on till I got away. While my superior muttered, 'Get her off me, Mary.' I collapsed, laughing. Disgusted, the would-be rescuer let go, spitting out, 'Well, you deserve everything they do to you now.'

Teaching at the Catholic Teachers College at the end of the 1970s brought the first experience of a Catholic prejudiced against religious. A former Sister from America attacked me for taking a job that a lay person could do. My subjects were Christian Morality and scripture, to qualify for which my congregation had sent me to gain a pontifical diploma and degree, undertaking that expense for the service of the Church. Now, but not in the 1970s, there are many laity capable of that role, but the attack is

*Matriculation girls, St Vincent's College, Sydney, 1910*

still unfair, because religious also need to earn their bread by the sweat of their brow. The resentment came because religious worked for a stipend, not a salary and so were more affordable.

Back to the present. Two years ago I was one of those talking to individual year 10 girls in my old school about how the place had changed. When chatting after the questions finished, my interviewer asked how many children I had. My eyebrows rose, and I said, 'But I'm a Sister!' She replied, 'Oh, aren't you allowed to get married?'

## Misunderstandings about religious life

Misunderstandings are nothing new. I kept quiet about entering, partly because I didn't plan to stay, and partly because everyone treated you as odd if you did. The automatic reaction was that I must have quarrelled with my dearly beloved: one friend told me that I needn't despair, that there would be others willing to have me, and that he wouldn't mind marrying me himself, if I couldn't find anyone else. Others told me that I wasn't the type, and so on. My mother accused me of laziness, selfishness and running away from responsibility. My only supporter, my brother, sat me down the night before I entered to explain that, even though in Ireland it would be a disgrace to leave the convent, any time I wanted to come back home, I would be welcomed.

So you can see, I'm not the ideal person to explain vocation. Some say that my usual contrariness made me enter. This is where I return to where I began: Not everything in life can be explained without admitting the supernatural. Now we'll try to say what religious life is.

## Definition

**St Paul's definition** was to call himself 'a slave of Jesus Christ, called to be an apostle, set apart for the gospel of God' (Rom 1:1). Today there are so many kinds of consecrated life that **church law** about it has to be general, so its **legal definition** begins: 'Life consecrated through profession of the evangelical counsels [i.e., chastity, poverty, obedience] is a stable form of living, in which the faithful follow Christ more closely under the action of the Holy Spirit, and are totally dedicated to God, who is supremely loved…'[3]

A more personal idea is to say that: **Religious life is a way of satisfying 'a hunger and a desire for a closer relationship with God.'**[4] The vicar for religious in Sydney, Sr Maria Casey RSJ, reminded us that 'the person in consecrated life responds to a call of the Spirit over and beyond' the 'baptismal call.'[5] A person won't stay happily unless an intimate relationship with God develops.

Someone may, of course, have a wrong motive, like: a friend who thought she'd look good in a habit, or a PNG non-Catholic national who explained that he went to the Catholic seminary because Catholic priests all drove Suzukis, or the young School Sister of Notre Dame in communist Yugoslavia who thought it was a guaranteed hundredfold investment that entitled her to a car of her own.[6]

## History of religious life

One reason that it's difficult to define religious life is that there have been, are, and will be, so **many different varieties**, many more than Mr Heinz ever thought of. We all know the old saying, that not even God knows how many groups of religious women there are. How did it all begin? In Jesus' time, those who followed Jesus most closely were his first permanent disciples, as well as the women who went with them, providing for them 'out of their resources' (Lk 8:3). After the resurrection, **widows** were devoted to the work of the gospel, for example, making clothes for the poor. **Virgins** were also consecrated, though Paul pointed out that they were free to marry if celibacy became too difficult (1 Cor 7:9). When the Roman empire became more degenerate, some Christians retreated to the desert in order to avoid temptation, and lived as **hermits**. Next, people lived in **groups**, gathered into *monasteries*, then, later, orders like Franciscans and Dominicans, as well as Jesuits, went around to preach and teach outside monasteries. In other words, **religious life kept adopting new ways to be better able to serve each new age**. The Sydney vicar for religious, Sr Maria Casey RSJ, could list groups in Australia that have permission for a different form of consecrated life, like the Missionaries of Divine Love, who include families.

Women like **Mary Ward**,[7] who tried to do the same as men, were blocked by the official Church's conviction that women were too weak to resist temptation if allowed outside the convent.[8] **St Vincent de Paul** managed to get around restrictions on his Daughters of Charity in France by saying that they weren't *really* religious. That allowed them to go out and help the poor. It wasn't until the nineteenth century that the **Sisters of Charity** in Ireland had a co-founder, Bishop (later Archbishop) **Daniel Murray**, stubborn enough to fight to have his institute of Sisters of Charity **allowed to have perpetual vows and yet** be **free from enclosure**, the novel 'walking nuns'.[9]

When asked to explain how we would help the poor, **Murray wished us to be 'extensively useful'**, that is to do whatever was needed, so we have never had just one type of work to do, but function more as scouts or trailblazers, a bit like migrants who do the jobs that others don't take.[10]

## Vocation

There will always be people whom God coaxes or obliges to make God the be all and end all of their lives. **It's about time to ask why people take on religious life.** In a jubilee homily on 20 February 2016, Fr Kevin Walsh likened vocation to dovetailing in carpentry: it's finding your exact fit.

**The answer is different for each.** Jeremiah and Francis Thompson answer for me. In Jeremiah's words [20:7]: 'O LORD, you have enticed me, and I was enticed, you have overpowered me, and you have prevailed.' Thompson imagined God as the pursuer, almost the greyhound chasing a live rabbit![11] That was more or less what I experienced: a nagging question about entering wouldn't stop.

On a human level there were many factors, including strong family faith, talks on Catholic Action from our Leaving Certificate teacher, the realisation that among the children of mixed or broken marriages in my class, few or none would be likely to enter, then the active Catholicism of the Newman Society with Fr Roger Pryke at University, and, perhaps, the word 'charity' in the name 'Sisters of Charity.' Because of the church I grew up in, there was even an element of the fear of hell. Graham Greene's biographer suggested that it was Greene's **weakness, rather than his strength**, that kept him Catholic.[12] I could say the same about my coming to religious life. Whatever the motive for entering, staying is a different decision, made because of relationship with God, one in which **God is always the Giver.**

**Professional life as a religious**

When I was professed, you could be sent to do anything, anywhere in the congregation. To my horror, just because I had a degree and had taught for a few weeks in the country with the Sisters of Mercy, I was told to begin the Leaving Certificate classes in Hurstville.

Sisters became used to being thrown into the deep end. If not a religious, I would never have had the confidence to do the tasks I was given. Religious life pushed me beyond my expectations. For me, it really was a case of 'Fools rush in where angels fear to tread.' The vow of obedience meant that you went ahead and did what you were told to do, even if it seemed impossible. My mother had worked somewhat on the same lines. If I ever said to her that I didn't know how to do something she asked, she would answer, 'Well, you won't learn any younger.' Religious life for me ended up with all kinds of incredible situations that I would never have ventured into on my own initiative, even to disagreeing face to face with the second in charge at the Vatican's Sacred Congregation for Religious and Secular Institutes. Those in charge of hospitals and other ministries would say the same about going beyond their imaginings, especially with finance. The then premier of NSW, Neville Wran, at the 1960 opening of the Cameron Wing of St Vincent's Hospital at Darlinghurst, said that if S M Bernice had been in charge of BHP it would never have run at a loss.

This could mean being out of my depth, as when a German cardinal staying in the same hostel wanted to meet the new Australian cardinal who was visiting. Flustered, I introduced the Australian as 'Cardinal Newman', and couldn't understand the strange look he gave me. Nevertheless, Cardinal Freeman included me in his family visit with Pope Paul VI, another unexpected meeting.

When I began teaching as a Sister in 1957, upper classes were small, and it was possible to know the girls well. Australian Church law at the time ordered Catholic parents to send children to Catholic schools. As Catholic children had no choice in the matter, we were morally obliged to give them as good, or a better education, than they could have anywhere else. It seems to me that independent schools and hospitals have an extra value in keeping standards high in the public system and are valuable to the nation, not just for co-religionists.

## Experiencing life as a religious

After considering vocation and work, today I want to describe how I found religious life from the inside. This was prompted by an ACHS member sounding amazed at how long I'd lasted. Actually, so am I. Considering that the day I went to the novitiate I was scolded by a Sister there for keeping Mother General waiting, and that I then refused to accept the name the Superior General wanted me to use, it's no wonder that I resolved to go home the same day if my mother asked me again.

Once professed, satisfaction depends on faithfulness to prayer as well as on what we are told to do. I was lucky to have fulfilling and interesting tasks all my life.

Another great help has been closeness to my priest brother and being involved with his parish interests and friends. As well, it gave me wonderful relaxation sailing with him. Even professionally, his friendship was useful. An Australian bishop had to examine me to judge if I was fit to teach at the Catholic Teachers' College, North Sydney. The examination consisted of chatting about his relatives in Ireland. The report presented apparently was: 'She's all right. I know her brother.'

Stronger than everything else, though, is the support we receive from each other in the congregation. It was almost palpable when I was working or studying outside Australia. Even though we don't all live in big communities any more, the enthusiasm when we meet shows that we don't lose our sense of togetherness and support, thank God.

## A memoir of the value of a religious life for one individual

Pictures can express better than words how our life has essentials and incidentals. Rogier van der Weyden's *Mary Magdalene*[13] illustrates Mary's devotion to prayer during her life. It does not mean to prove that books existed in first century Palestine. A photo of junior university candidates at St Vincent's College in 1910 presents a cluster of girls in cluttered costumes. No principal today expects schoolgirls to wear what they wore in 1910, so why do some expect religious women to wear the multiple layers and torture headgear of 1815? These hospital Sisters photographed in 1895 give some idea of the multiple layers in religious habits.

*The author with Pope Paul VI, Cardinal James Freeman, Mons. James Madden, Rome, 1973*

Because we religious are people of our time and our background, incidentals like dress will change from time to time. Times change. We are now shocked to learn that there used to be **lay Sisters** in our congregations, ones who did the housekeeping and other tasks in the big communities, freeing the rest to teach or nurse or do visitation. Just as the New Testament takes slavery for granted, the nineteenth century assumed that lay Sisters, equivalent to the servants those Sisters had in their homes, would do all the domestic work.[14] Pius XII and Vatican II reminded religious that all are equal, and lay Sisters were integrated with the choir Sisters, DG.

Dress or habit was similarly a part of the original era of the congregation's founding. Sisters of Charity adopted one like that worn by widows in nineteenth century Ireland. It was never practical for Australia, but much less so in the twentieth century. Sisters no longer have the leisure or skills to make their habits or to maintain the starching and ironing needed. Serge became impossibly costly and then unobtainable. On the other hand, shops have less expensive clothes. Yet that change from habits upset many inside and outside. 'You used to look so lovely in your habits' summarises what some Catholics saw as the value of religious women.

The move into ordinary dress after Vatican II was also a sign of the times: that the ME age had arrived, the age when each wanted to express her individuality, not hide it under a uniform. Those of you who remember habits will know how hard it was sometimes was to know one from another. A father once embraced a Sister from behind, then discovered she was not his daughter.

When we Sisters of Charity changed, we changed bit by bit. The first raising of the hem to mid-calf and showing a 'token' of hair came when I was teaching at a co-ed secondary school at Katoomba in 1969. There was a stunned silence at the lines assembled before school when the pupils first saw the new fashion. They mobilised their energies by the time of the morning break assembly and the boys greeted us with wolf whistles. That was not written in the convent *Annals*.

**Convent life in the 1950s was circumscribed.** Junior Sisters were not allowed to read newspapers or novels or use the phone without permission. In my first community there was an elderly Sister, a music teacher, who used to corner me in a discreet spot, hand me a brown paper bag, saying, "Mary, all the girls are reading this. You should know what they're reading, but don't let anyone see you with it.' The only visitors we were allowed usually were family members, and then no more than once a month. One superior didn't allow me to speak to girls' parents when they phoned.

We didn't eat with non-religious, even in our own homes, and had to ask for money for fares or anything else. At Christmas once, staying at another convent, I shocked the superior by telling her that, since my convent didn't have an account at the bookshop, I had charged a textbook I needed to hers. Initiatives like that were NOT encouraged.

In the 1950s, there were no free periods, so preparing classes was all done at night. In Tasmania, the school was so poor that the younger Sisters, on top of teaching and all duties in the convent, looked after the grounds, mowed the extensive lawns, cared for the flower gardens, and cleaned every part of the school, including the boys' toilets. One girl there said she gave up the idea of entering because Sisters had to work too hard. That sounds grim, but Sisters made their own fun.

In Tasmania, because there were relatively few schools, I was on several syllabus or examination boards. My favourite was one for ABC radio language programmes. All the other members were male and so they always gave me the one comfortable chair!

**On-going development**

Seven years spent in Tasmania in **Archbishop Guilford Young's** time were a great blessing. By his command, we had Saturday afternoon updating sessions on scripture and the sacraments. He also prepared the priests, who prepared the people, for Vatican II's liturgical changes. We were eventually so weary of being prepared that we couldn't wait for the changes to come, whereas in some other States people were just hit with them.

A book showing how Vatican II changes impacted on English converts to Catholicism[15] brought home to me how their experiences of the changes, and their feelings of disappointment and betrayal, resemble those of Catholics unprepared for Vatican II's return to original rites and new interpretations. These reactions are also like what happened with some religious – and even priests – with renewal and adaptation. Resisters to what they saw as new ideas sincerely thought that change was wrong. [16]

Those of us who were teachers had updating in both education and religion from Catholic education offices and other trained individuals, that is, more opportunities than others had. A former seminarian asked me in a card, after he had been ordained some years,: 'Are you still trying to break open closed minds?'

That more or less encapsulates much of my development and renewal: breaking open my own closed mind and helping others to do the same. It could not have happened without our chaplain at university, Father Roger Pryke, Archbishop Young, and the opportunity my Congregation gave me of four years of study in Rome. That also allowed me to make new friends in Rome, and also when I used a Jesuit library in France for two months.

## Today's religious life

Perhaps **emphasis on the Holy Spirit in each believer** has most responsibility for what has happened in religious institutes. Instead of the superior thinking that she alone has a direct line to God, we now acknowledge that God speaks to all who are willing to listen. We talk now about shared responsibility, since each has wisdom within. After Vatican II, there have been fewer square pegs in round holes.

Forbidden words, like **initiative and new ideas**, suddenly became kosher. There are some religious still somewhat institutionalised mentally, but they are rarer. Many Sisters live in clusters, which gives them the freedom they need for a particular task but offers support as well. Some of us still live in community. Physical separateness is not important when we are close spiritually and and emotionally. A benefit of the decline in the numbers of religious is that we share more with other congregations, both for formation programmes and also in apostolic works. A great joy is realising that we are part of the laity, and also that we have led others to take over many of our initiatives.

**Envoi**

During World War II some of us as girls used to help an old Sister on Saturdays bake and pack hosts for the American troops in the Pacific, and the convent was always silent. In our family home we sang as we did the housework, so I decided that the Sisters were all unhappy, seeing that they kept quiet and didn't sing as they worked. Entering the convent was to accept a sorrowful life. I couldn't have been more wrong. Now I shudder when I think of the mess I would have made of life, if I had not entered. Far from being unhappy, a life for God meant the delight of teaching, being enriched by non-stop learning, and the joy of making friends in so many areas. *Magnificat anima Dominum.*

**Question time**

Q. What was the title of the book in the brown paper bag?

A. It was *The Nun's Story*, showing as a film then with Deborah Kerr. [A missionary sister in the Belgian Congo, unhappy, falls in love with a doctor and leaves the convent.]

Q. What was it about your time in Rome that most opened your mind?

A. Studying theology and church history, and finding that there were different theologies in favour at different eras of the Church, so that those frowned on in one generation could be rehabilitated in another. This was a shock to someone raised thinking that the green catechism's answers were the only way in which truth could be framed.

Q. Why did you personally see change as necessary?

A. My natural instinct is to ask 'Why?', if change is proposed. I have to be convinced that it's necessary, helpful, and right.[I was also impressed by a talk by Fr Jerome Murphy-O'Connor O.P. at Santa Sabina, when he stressed the dangers of disunion if changes were made insensitively, without bringing as many as possible to accept they were necessary.]

Q. Many religious left in the 1970s. What was the impact? Were there any scandals like the early Ligouri one?

A. The first reaction was pain at losing them. However, it was a good decision for most, who had been too young when entering to know what they were doing. Others were frustrated by institutes' slowness to obey church directives to update. Some had unfortunate experiences with superiors who overstepped their authority. We are able to keep in touch with many, some help in our ministries and send their children to our schools. [Many who left worked for the Church, making us grateful for the years they gave us, as well as proud of what they did afterwards.]

## Notes

1. Cf. the comment made by Dr Lesley Hughes on early writings of religious women, in her 2002 thesis, *To Labour Seriously: Catholic Sisters and Social Welfare in late nineteenth century Sydney.*
2. This novel won the Man Booker prize in 2013.
3. These are the opening words of canon 583#1, *The Code of Canon Law in English Translation* (London: Collins, 1983, 1984), 105.
4. The *Catholic Weekly*, 13 September 2015, 15, gives this explanation of his vocation from Jack O'Sullivan FMS, on his first profession: 'Participating in three World Youth Days and animating youth groups in parishes left me with a hunger and a desire for a closer relationship with God.'
5. Maria Casey, in a talk on the meaning of Pope Francis' letter on consecrated life, given at a Broken Bay Institute conference at Baulkham Hills, 11 August 2015. Text supplied by Sr Maryanne Confoy, RSC, moderator.
6. This was a story told to me by the former bursar of the School Sisters of Notre Dame that she heard when visiting Yugoslavia after the fall of the Iron Curtain.
7. 1585-1645
8. Comments like this were in the objections raised against the original constitutions of the Irish Sisters of Charity, held in the archives of the Sacred Congregation of Propaganda.
9. For the story of religious women in Australia, see Rosa MacGinley, *A Dynamic of Hope: Institutes of Women Religious in Australia* (Sydney: Crossing Press, 1996).
10. The words are from Murray's letter to Aikenhead, 6 December 1815, describing the wording of the Sisters' fourth vow, that of service of the poor, 'in the manner that we all agreed upon as the best to render the congregation extensively useful.' Taken from S. [Sarah] A.[Atkinson], *Mary Aikenhead: Her Life, Her Work, and Her Friends* (Dublin: Browne & Nolan, 1911), 151.
11. Francis Thompson, *The Hound of Heaven.*
12. Quoted in Joseph Pearce, *Literary Converts: Spiritual Inspiration in an Age of Unbelief* (London: HarperCollins, 1999), 424-5. [Cf. Nellie Aloysius: 'Mary, you know I don't like the Charities, but even I wouldn't wish that on them.']
13. 1390/1400-1464.
14. See Caitriona Clear, *Nuns in Nineteenth Century Ireland* (Dublin: Gill and Macmillan, 1987).
15. Pearce, op.cit..
16. Cf. Machiavelli's explanation of resistance to change: 'the reformer has enemies in all those who profit by the old order, and only lukewarm defenders in all those who would profit by the new order ... who do not truly believe in anything new until they have had actual experience of it', Niccolo Machiavelli, *The Prince* (New York: Modern Library, 1940), p.21, quoted in Doris Kearns Goodwin, *Lyndon Johnson and the American Dream* (New York: St Martin's Griffin, 1976, 1991, p.112.

**Some reading:**

Margaret Beirne, RSC, '"Old Habits Die Hard": The Experience of Australian Religious Women in the Wake of Vatican II', in Neil Ormerod et al., *Vatican II: Reception and Implementation in the Australian Church* (Mulgrave, Vic.: Australian Catholic University, 2012), 154-175.

Walter Brueggemann, 'A Call to Leaders,' ch.7, *Transformational Leadership: Conversations with the Leadership Conference of Women Religious*, ed. Annmarie Sanders (Maryknoll, NY: Orbis Books, 2015.

Robyn Cadwallader, *The Anchoress* (Sydney: Fourth Estate, 2015), for a modern writer who imagines the thinking of a hermit.

Caitriona Clear, *Nuns in Nineteenth Century Ireland* (Dublin: Gill and Macmillan, 1987).

Broken Bay Institute Conference on Pope Francis, 'Letter on Consecrated Life', 11 August 2015.

*Catholic Weekly* of 13 September 2015, report of Marist Brothers profession ceremony.

*The Code of Canon Law in English Translation* (London: Collins, 1983, 1984) 105, canon 583#1.

Rosa MacGinley, *A Dynamic of Hope: Institutes of Women Religious in Australia* (Sydney: Crossing Press, 1996).

Heather O'Connor, *The Challenge of Change: Mercy and Loreto Sisters in Ballarat 1950-1980* (Ballan, Australia: Connor Court Publishing, 2013).

Joseph Pearce, *Literary Converts: Spiritual Inspiration in an Age of Unbelief* (London: HarperCollins 1999).

## Book Review

*150 years on Pyrmont Peninsula: The Catholic Community of St Bede, 1867-2017*

Author: C F Fowler
Publisher: ATF Publishing, South Australia, 2017
ISBN: 1925486877, 9781925486872
Paperback: $35.00

Reviewed by: Damian John Gleeson*

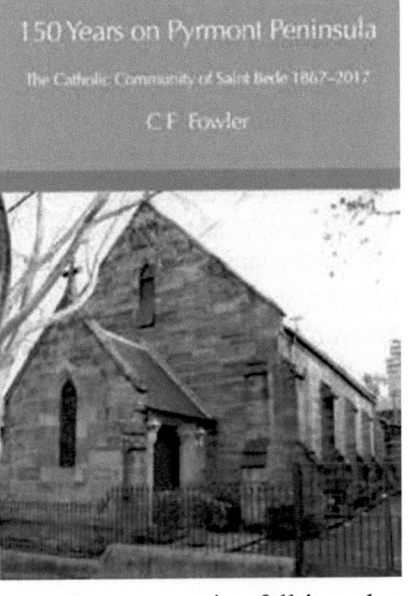

Within the emerging genre of professional parish historiography a number of works have recently been produced, including this extensive history of probably Sydney's smallest church, St Bede's, and the history of the vibrant Catholic communities of Ultimo and Pyrmont.

The author, Dr Colin Fowler, a former Pyrmont Parish Priest, has researched and produced a splendid history, which is strongly contextualised within the framework, and at times, vagaries, of Archdiocesan history and politics.

A critic might suggest that the book reflects a first-class PhD thesis, as it is work of great labour. This lengthy tome of 25 chapters is not for the faint hearted; not that generations of Pyrmont's congregation fall into that category.

*150 years on Pyrmont Peninsula* begins with a detailed history of Pyrmont as a suburb and places early Catholic developments within the 'mother' parish of St Benedict's Church, George Street West (now Broadway). The reader, though, is left with a feeling that there might have

---

* Damian John Gleeson PhD, a past President of the Australian Catholic Historical Society, wrote a history of St Martha's Parish.

been more contrast made between the Irish-Australian communities of Broadway and Pyrmont. Even today, Broadway has an air of superiority, unlike the more grounded Pyrmont community.

The 19th century Irishness of Pyrmont was dissimilar to Broadway and indeed most Sydney parishes, because Pyrmont did not resemble a traditional parish dominated by Tipperary, Clare and Limerick migrants. Dr Fowler skillfully examines the non-Munster (O') Toole families of Wexford and Wicklow, who played a critical role in the development of St Bede's. While I cannot recall a parish history that devotes so much attention to one family, this level of focus become readily appropriate. It is a remarkable story, well beyond the confines of genealogical interest. Readers will be fascinated by the unmasking of the first O'Toole, Patrick, as both Pyrmont's chief Catholic fundraiser/treasurer and his unabashed membership of a secret masonic-style society. By 20th century prohibition standards such dualism may have been sufficient for excommunication, but Patrick O'Toole followed a growing Irish precedence which the Catholic Church tolerated until Cardinal Cullen replaced pragmatism with dogmatism.

*150 years on Pyrmont Peninsula* transparently examines the sad lives of many clergy sent to Pyrmont, often in retribution for perceived or actual disobedience. Perhaps the strongest example was Fr Michael McNamara, who despite significant achievements in the turbulent Hurstville-Kogarah-Rockdale Mission, became unfairly embroiled in the Coningham affair and was demoted to be a curate at Pyrmont. Loneliness of clerical life, and reliance on alcohol and gambling, compounded in financial irregularities during Fr Michael O'Connell's pastorship, notwithstanding his determination to improve school facilities in what was a materially poor parish.

The author relies to a large extent on official documents and newspaper coverage in a most detailed assessment of St Bede's. There is solid coverage of the Good Samaritan Sisters, and in the latter decades of the twentieth century the ebbs and flows of Pyrmont being the port chaplaincy.

The parish's decline and revival are also well covered as the author carefully sifts through the impact of shortsighted Archdiocesan decisions. A priestless Catholic community was one of several poor decisions, given that at the time Pyrmont's long anticipated tremendous population growth had already begun, and there was a reasonable supply of locally-born clergy. Pyrmont today is one of the most densely populated suburbs in Australia.

The book has a few surprises. An absence of photos in the main text, explained in terms of a paucity of photos, may however disappoint some readers. The absence, however, has been partially offset by the appendix, which includes a reprint of the small centenary parish history. This publishing choice may have merit given the 1967 booklet is out of print, but it is hoped that such a trend is not automatically replicated in future historiography.

Ecumenical vignettes, rare to be found in a parish history, are applauded. Despite the length, there are only a few typographical errors (mainly in the index) which reflects the writer's diligence. Indeed, it is most pleasing to see an index, something rare in Catholic parish histories. The author, to his credit, has made the additional effort of including a person's occupation in entries. However, the index is slightly weakened by not including events and institutions.

Dr Fowler's work sets a high mark in Catholic historiography. This book will appeal to a wide cross section, including tertiary and seminary students, clergy, laity, inner city communities, and descendants of pioneer families. The St Bede's Catholic community can be justly proud that they are the recipients of such tremendous scholarship.

## BOOK REVIEW

*Santamaria: A most unusual man*

Author: Gerard Henderson
Publisher: Miegunyah Press, 2015
ISBN: 9780522868586
Hardback, 505 pages, $59.99

Book review by James Franklin*

Controversy about B A Santamaria may die down when everyone passionately involved with his life and ideas is dead. That will be some time yet. In the meantime, all sides will welcome Henderson's well-informed, accurate, and generally fair account.

Santamaria was on the right side of the main international political issue of his time, the threat of Communism. He devoted his immense intellectual and organizational skills to combatting it, in an atmosphere where many were either stupidly blind to the threat or criminally covering it up. If he

*James Franklin is editor of the *Journal of the Australian Catholic Historical Society.*

had lived in Czechoslovakia or Vietnam – or if he had died in 1950 – his alarmist views would have been vindicated in full and his actions proven to be justified. The question is whether the rising prosperity and political stability of 1950s Australia rendered his apocalyptic vision out of date and his infiltration of the Labor Party morally improper. It is easy to see why Stalin with an H-bomb and Evatt's office with communist moles were still cause for worry. It is equally easy to see the point of view of traditional anti-communist Labor men like Calwell who thought no good could come of single-issue conspiratorial tactics. Henderson's careful account lays out the facts as clearly and comprehensively as can be done at this stage. He is particularly strong on the ins and outs of political issues and strategies and on clearing away myths that have arisen. Readers can make their own judgements.

Santamaria as man of ideas is not quite so clear in the book. That is not for lack of basic raw material – perhaps no Australian expounded such a huge and varied stream of closely-argued positions over so many decades. But Santamaria himself gave the impression that he did all his serious thinking when young, and adopted a position that then required only tactical changes and decoration with current references for the rest of his life. All his effort could then go into organization and propaganda. Since everything he wrote was with an eye for its political effect, it is not easy for a biographer to work out what he really believed.

That is particularly so with Santamaria's relation to his Catholic faith. He was seen and saw himself as staunchly and militantly Catholic. But the vision of Catholicism he absorbed from his mentor Archbishop Mannix involved certain departures from the mainstream. Indeed, it was Santamaria's own book about Mannix that revealed the extraordinary extent of Mannix's defiance of Vatican directives with which he disagreed. Santamaria persisently evaded Vatican orders in the late 1950s concerning the separation of Church and state. But come 1968, no-one was more enthusiastic than him in defending *Humanae Vitae* and demanding loyalty to the Pope's teaching. In his pamphlet *Contraception* (Henderson calls it

"Santa's very own encyclical"), he wrote "If [anyone] proposes to remain a member, he accepts the decisions of its governing body. If he finds those decisions shocking to his conscience, he has the courage of his convictions and leaves the organisation." When Santamaria became deeply unhappy with the directions the Church took after the Second Vatican Council, he set up the magazine *AD2000* to turn back the tide. Santamaria's attitude resembles that of Pope Francis's recent conservative critics: loyalty to the Pope is for when the Pope agrees with me.

One regrettable lacuna in the book is the story of why Santamaria and Henderson fell out, after working closely for some years around 1970. In general terms, the answer is obvious – they were both "I did it my way" personalities and no organization was going to be big enough for both of them. But the exact first-hand story of what happened would have been entertaining.

In researching the biography, Henderson did not have the cooperation of Santamaria's family. His book is the last word on Santamaria on the evidence now available. It may not be the last word if the family releases more documents to a sympathetic biographer.

## BOOK REVIEW

*Australian Religious Thought*

Author: Wayne Hudson
Publisher: Monash University Publishing, 2016
ISBN: 9781922235763
Paperback, 248 pages, $22.95

Book review by James Franklin*

This is an excellent and hugely informative book on its topic. But its topic is not exactly Australian religious thought. It is mainly about Australian semi-religious thought, or unorthodox religious thought, or original religious thought, or sometimes, hardly-at-all-religious thought. Most readers will be astonished at the inventiveness of the vast range of Australian religious thinkers that Hudson has dug up, and grateful for his mostly thumbnail

*James Franklin is the author of *Corrupting the Youth: A history of philosophy in Australia* (Macleay Press, 2003).

## AUSTRALIAN RELIGIOUS THOUGHT
### WAYNE HUDSON

sketches of what they said. But as one of the points of religion (in contrast to philosophy) is to think in fidelity with some tradition, the result is a strangely skewed view of what has been thought by religious people in Australia. Hudson seems inclined to think that if someone is orthodox they are merely parrotting a party line and not really thinking. That underplays the ability of quite strict orthodoxies to have something new to say.

Hudson usefully distinguishes between "unbelief", a lack of belief possibly accompanied by regret and some sympathy or nostalgia for religion, and "disbelief", a positive anti-belief often accompanied by hostility to religion. While both have existed in Australia, he points out that this country has lacked the violent hostility to religion common in Latin countries, possibly matching the lack of extreme views on the religious side. The Australian Catholic Church, a large and eventually the largest denomination and politically powerful, has shown no ambition to make Australia a confessional state. B.A. Santamaria had extensive, some would say overweening, political ambitions, but he did not want to become Franco.

On specifically Catholic themes, Hudson gives respectful treatment to the scholastic philosophy that underpinned seminary training, moral theory and apologetics from the late nineteenth century to the 1960s. The poets Francis Webb, James McAuley and Les Murray are said to combine elements of faith and disbelief, as are the neurophysiologist Sir John Eccles and B.A. Santamaria. That is a reasonable view as those figures, even in periods of their lives when they claimed to be fully orthodox, remained independent-minded in ways that in other contexts might have attracted accusations of "cafeteria Catholicism". Regrettably missing is any mention of the more definitely orthodox Archbishop Mannix and Arthur Calwell, whose reading of *Rerum Novarum* informed a particular theory of political action, one that provided an influential alternative and counterbalance to the Marxist vision that in the mid-twentieth century threatened to dominate left-wing politics. Also absent is the intellectual field in which Australian Catholic thought has probably been strongest, history. Patrick O'Farrell and other historians are not mentioned.

In the chapter on theology, where orthodoxy does have a higher profile than elsewhere in the book, evangelicals such as Broughton Knox are given more prominence than Catholics. However post-Vatican II Catholic theology is treated sympathetically, with its developments in the Trinity and Christology by such theologians as David Coffey, Anthony Kelly, Gerald O'Collins and Neil Ormerod.

Still, the main point of the book is its accounts not of institutionalised church-supported thinking but of, so to speak, DIY religion. Theosophy. Pantheism. Process theology. Spiritualism. Unitarianism. Pantheism. The union movement ("Trades unionism is a new and grand religion": Henry Lawson). Personal "explorations" of the divine. You name it.

Interesting as these ideas often were, the outside observer may wonder if the whole project was getting anywhere. Unorthodox religious thinkers appear from this account to have been sincere and often intelligent seekers after the truth, and their complaints about the rigidities, narrowness and power obsessions of the institutional churches were often justified, but their alternatives are often hard to understand. A power beyond our ken, what does that mean? With a theology involving a personal God, we at least know where we are, but it is often hard to see what unorthodox thinkers believe the contents of the universe actually are. The Sydney process theologian and biologist Charles Birch, for example, is said to believe in a God as the "cosmic mind, or within of all things", which "did not intervene in the world, but acted on all entities by persuasion and feeling". Easy to say, but does the combination of words mean anything?

These trends also find it hard to match traditional religions in the institutional and social roles of religion. Not for want of trying, but the farcical results can be seen in the new "Beatitudes" devised for the Spiritualist Sunday Schools of Victoria in 1877 by the Spiritualists' president, Alfred Deakin:

*Conductor.* – Blessed are the dutiful;
*Leaders.* – For they shall find the peace which cannot be bought and sold.
*Conductor.* – Blessed are the punctual.
*Children.* – For they have learned the lesson which the stars and planets teach ...
*Conductor.* – Blessed are the faithful, the dutiful, the punctual, the orderly, the innocent, the pure in heart;
*All.* – For theirs is the republic of heaven.

If you're going to have a religion, you might as well have a real one.

BOOK REVIEW

*Armour of Light: The stained glass windows of St James' Church, Forest Lodge, those to whom they are dedicated and their families*

Author: Anne Wark
Publisher: Parish of St James, Forest Lodge 2010
ISBN: 9780646540801
Paperback, 133 pages, $20.00 from National Trust Shop

Book review by Max Solling*

On 1 September 1878 Archbishop Polding consecrated St James' Church, named after the apostle called from his fishing to follow Christ. Church building in Glebe made architects and builders rich, and in the 1880s all major Christian denominations, except the Baptists, had their own places of worship in Glebe. As the churches represented the largest voluntary grouping in colonial society they exercised a powerful pervasive influence on the conduct of life.

A sure sign of Catholic fidelity was the way they supported their schools – St James' (1880), St Ita's (1900) and St Scholastica's (1902) and strong networks were established around the church where they worshipped, educated their children and sought fellowship. An integral part of these networks were the Good Samaritan Sisters and the Patrician Brothers. St James is a place where local people are baptised, married and mourned as they embark on their last journey; a place where the sense of family and local piety is given tangible form.

*Max Solling is the author of histories of Glebe and Leichhardt.

## Armour of Light: The stained glass windows of St James' Church, Forest Lodge

St James has been a thriving parish for more than 130 years, and its history was first explored by John Fletcher in 1977 and brought up to date by Michael Hogan in 2002.[1] Anne Wark's *Armour of Light* is a wonderful addition to these two works, shedding much light on the stained glass windows of St James and the people to whom the windows are dedicated.

In 1878 the church contained stained glass windows in the sanctuary in memory of James Doheny, John Morris, Flora Morris and John Young beside artistic depictions of St James and St John. The side windows were in leadlight with clear diamond shaped panes of glass. Ove the next thirty years or so, these windows were replaced with beautifully wrought stained glass donated by individuals or families in memory of loved ones and reflecting the spirituality of the church of the day. They were constructed in Sydney by artisans John Falconer and Frederick Ashwin in partnership with John Radecki who became one of Ashwin's chief designers.

What do we know of the kind of parishioners who attended St James during the time these windows were added? The marriage register of St James reveals 450 marriages took place in the church between 1878 and 1897 with a strong representation of Irish-born brides and grooms. The largest number of these emigrants came from counties Clare, Cork, Limerick, Tipperary and Donegal, with Cavan, Kerry, Mayo, Meath, Tyrone and Kilkenny less common. Prominent among the occupations of St James grooms were labourers and cabmen together with innkeeper, carpenter and upholsterer, tending to support Cardinal Moran's observation in his massive 1895 history that Irish Catholics were concentrated among the landless, unskilled labouring class. Catholics retained a self-image of being drinkers according to Patrick O'Farrell but parishioners at Forest Lodge were proud of their 120 member Total Abstinence Association, formed in 1888; it met monthly to renew the pledge, listen to readings and sing songs.

*Armour of Light* restores the identity and character to people who left little written record of their lives, their original importance. In 1904, for example, a devoted wife donated a window in memory of her husband Carl Carlson, born in Sweden about 1837 and who came ashore in Sydney as a 25-year-old. Shortly after he married Irish girl Catherine Gallagher, neither able to sign their name, giving their assent with an 'X'. However during the 1860s literacy greatly improved with nearly two-thirds of both sexes being able to read and write. The energetic and entrepreneurial Carlson quickly learned the ways of the prevailing Anglo-Celtic culture, bought and sold town property and prospered in his new land. He helped establish the Scandinavian Seamen's Home in the Rocks and moved to 270 Glebe Road in 1902, dying there two years later. A particularly poignant and beautiful window is dedicated to the Irish National Foresters' Benefit Society, a benevolent society with nationalist ideals, united by a common desire to assist members in hard times. Without the sustaining services of a welfare state, the Society offered a measure of protection to working families during periods of illness, unemployment and old age.

*Armour of Light* is a little gem of suburban history, a meticulously researched and insightful labour of love. It is complete with a Glebe map indicating where the people identified in the windows lived, a church floor plan, footnotes, bibliography and above all its beautifully illustrated stained glass windows, some of the church's richest treasures. The publishers are to be congratulated for producing such a handsome book.

**Notes**
1 John Fletcher with additional material by Michael Hogan, *St James' Parish, Forest Lodge: 125 years: 1877-2002*, Michael Hogan, Forest Lodge, 2002.

**BOOK REVIEW**

*When We Are Weak, Then We Are Strong: A History of the Marist Sisters in Australia 1907 – 1984*

Author: Joan C McBride, sm
Publisher: Marist Sisters, 2006
ISBN: 9780646468075
Paperback, 196 pages, $44.00

Reviewed by Robyn Dunlop*

Commissioned by the Marist Provincial of Australia and written by Joan McBride, sm, *When We Are Weak, Then We Are Strong* is a record of the presence and activities of the Marist Sisters in Australia in the twentieth century.

The book has been written for the "next generation" of Marist Sisters, in what is now the Asia-Pacific Region of the Order. Times have changed, as the name of the new Region indicates; Australia is not where the new

* Dr Robyn Dunlop is a historian and author of *Planted in Congenial Soil: The Diocesan Sisters of St Joseph, Lochinvar, 1883 – 1917*.

novices are coming from today. The future Sisters, "who will be living in a very different world from that of our early sisters, will learn nevertheless to find much strength from those who have gone before them". McBride includes in her focus some challenging and "less edifying moments", but her emphasis is on episodes from which future Marists can take courage from.

McBride provides helpful background sketches to the founding of the Order in France, the difficulties the Marists faced in France in the late 1800s and early 1900s, and to Catholic and state education in Australia. From there, she begins to document in chronological order the major events involving Marist Sisters in Australia.

The work suggests broader themes worth considering in historical work on religious institutions. The economics involved in shaping outcomes, for instance. The first Marist Sisters to mission in Fiji in 1892, came from France. Due to the expense involved in getting Sisters from Europe to Fiji, a house in Australia began to be discussed as a better (cheaper, quicker) option for getting subjects for Fiji missions. The Sisters in Australia had to support themselves (unlike those in Fiji), so to supplement the meagre income they made from running a primary school, the early Marist Sisters in Woolwich, Sydney, taught music and French after school hours and moves were soon made to open a "high" (fee-paying) school that took boarders.

The physical and personal costs to the Sisters themselves is another theme that appears. The early Marist Sisters who went to Fiji encountered typhoid, tuberculosis and physical vulnerabilities in a new climate that had long-term – sometimes fatal – consequences. The founding Marist Community in Australia was only made up of three Sisters, and one was so homesick for Europe – McBride suggests – that she was very difficult to get along with, often spending days in bed and belittling her Superior in front of others (the third member of the household spoke little English – mainly French – and was going deaf). Later, during World War I and II, Sisters in Oceania were without communication with family and communities in Europe, sometimes for years. What toll did this take?

The Marist Sisters were at a disadvantage when they first came to Australia for they had no administrative authority here. The Archbishop of Sydney (Kelly) kept a very close eye on the Sisters, at times ignoring their Pontifical status and personally questioning the running of their Novitiate. The relationships between female Religious Orders and Bishops in Australia have never been easy and this one does not inspire.

One feature that set the Marist Sisters in Australia apart from other religious teaching Orders were their missions. Sisters were trained in Sydney before going to places like Fiji, Tonga and New Zealand, and mission Sisters would come back to Sydney for medical treatment and to recuperate. The Sisters were also in close contact with Marist Bishops and priests who were missioning in Oceania, and the men would often visit when in Sydney and talk to the students about their work. This formed "an outward vision" that was a significant part of the Marist culture.

The evacuation of the Woolwich school and novitiate to Mittagong in the Southern Highlands of NSW during WWII is detailed, followed by the expansion of schools in the 1950s and 1960s with the influx of migrants to Australia and the population boom at this time. The Marist Sisters' focus began to be more on Australia than missions.

An unexpected discovery are the numerous connections between the Marists and the Sisters of St Joseph of the Sacred Heart. Among others: the Marist Sisters' first school was founded by the Sisters of St Joseph (who only left it when it burned down), and in the 1950s, the Marist Sisters began to attend the Josephites' teacher training establishment in North Sydney.

As with other Religious Orders, from Vatican II there were changes in Community numbers (up, and then down) and variations in ministries. As Sisters aged, and the average age of Sisters increased, discussions of retirement and providing for elderly Sisters arose. At the same time as they were opening a retirement home, the Marist Sisters were looking outwards and an Australian Sister joined a new Marist Sister mission in Latin America. Both of these trends have continued – the ageing of the Sisters, and the participation in new missions with Marist Sisters from other countries.

The book includes short biographies of Sisters with notable connections to Australia. Appendices are somewhat confusing, giving religious and family names of Sisters but no information about their countries of origin, or dates of entry/departure/death. There are also lists of school principals (by state and school), and leaders.

**Author Statement:**

I would like to thank Dr Dunlop for her work. I was happy to see that she alluded to the "outward vision" that was and is so much part of our Marist culture.

I wish to advise that my book was written only for the Marist Sisters and not for general reading. For that reason, there are sections in the book, especially the latter part, which are for their information. The Appendices were added to help our sisters, who are in many different countries in the world, to identify the sisters in the book, many of whom they would have known under other names.

However, if anyone wants a copy of the book, they can apply to the Marist Sisters at Haberfield.

Sr Joan McBride sm

## Book Review

*Aquinas Academy 1945-2015 – A Very Personal Australian Story*

Author: Julie Thorpe
Publisher: ATF Theology Press, Adelaide, 2016
ISBN: 9781925486148
Binding: Paperback
Price: $29.95

Reviewed by Xavier Symons[*]

The Aquinas Academy of 2016 is very different institution from the Academy established in 1945. In the times of Rev Dr Austin Woodbury (affectionately known as 'The Doc'), the Sydney Academy offered generalised courses in Thomistic philosophy and theology, and these were taught with the systematic precision characteristic of the late 19th early 20th century manualist tradition. In contrast, the Academy today offers courses on spirituality, mysticism and comparative religion, and has a pedagogical style reflective of Post Vatican II theology – 'freedom of the spirit in the Spirit'. Prima facie, there are few traces left of the original Academy, save the odd photo of The Doc on the display in the historic Harrington Street classrooms.

Yet there is an amazing and complex history to this unique institution, and what exists today is arguably a reflection of the spirit of enquiry and love of wisdom that Austin Woodbury taught students all those years ago.

[*]Xavier Symons is a Research Associate at the Institute for Ethics and Society, University of Notre Dame, xavier.symons@nd.edu.au

Australian historian Julie Thorpe was commissioned with the difficult task of piecing together a rich tapestry of narratives – stories from former students both lay and religious, senior figures in the Church in Sydney from the 1930s until today, relatives and friends of the Doc, and most importantly, the various faculty members who have taught at the institution since its inception. *The Aquinas Academy 1945-2015 – A very personal Australian Story* is a delightful and engaging history that gives readers a window into the heart and mind of Austin Woodbury, and also those who succeeded him. The book is not a history of ideas or Catholic philosophy; it is, rather, a deeply personal history, and one that will be of great interest to anyone who has come in contact with the Academy over the years.

Julie Thorpe deftly condenses 70 years of history into very readable 160-page volume. Roughly half of the book deals with the life of Austin Woodbury, and the rapid development of the Academy in the late 1940s to early 1960s. Thorpe pays significant attention to Woodbury's personal history, and in particular early events in his life that left an indelible mark on his character and led him to immerse himself almost completely in his academic pursuits. The second half of the book discusses the transition of the academy from an exclusive focus on scholasticism to a Post-Vatican II focus on pastoral studies and mysticism. The Academy shifted its attention away from Woodbury's Thomism and toward Jungian psychanalysis and courses in pastoral theology. There were signs of a change in the direction at the academy following the end of Vatican II in 1965, and what were mere auspices soon became an inexorable force when the Doc stepped down as principal of Academy in 1974. Thorpe discusses the how Woodbury's preoccupation with pontifically recognised philosophy degrees was replaced with the desire of subsequent principals to offer 'Christian Growth Programs' for lay men and women.

It would not do Julie's book justice to ignore her very personal and endearing approach to writing history. To my mind this book is just as much reflective of Julie's uncanny sensitivity to the complexity of life as it is the rich personalities of characters like Austin Woodbury. In a sense Julie represents the lay, female audience for whom the academy today offers so much promise. And all this even in what appears to be – to use a concept from the German sociologist Max Weber – a thoroughly disenchanted world.

Each chapter of the book interweaves historical reflections with inteviews with significant figures associated with the academy. Julie clearly worked extremely hard to arrange some of these interviews – just wait till you read about her encounter with unionist and former politician Johno Johnson! The discussions are recounted in a lively style, and Julie skilfully captures the complex personalities and personal histories of these different significant figures in the history of the academy.

Thorpe is sympathetic to the new direction followed by the Academy in its post-Woodbury era. There are many who would not take so kindly to the Academy's current ethos (indeed, a splinter institute, the Centre for Thomistic Studies, still exists today, staffed by former students of Woodbury who disagree with the liberal approach to theology in the Academy). But while many are critical of the 'progressive' theology taught at the Academy today, there is general agreement – both among so-called liberals and conservatives – about the significant contribution that Woodbury made to Catholic intellectual life in Australia in the $20^{th}$ century. The sections of the book focused on Woodbury transcend to some extent the ideological divides that polarise Catholic theology and philosophy today. This is one of the book's strengths.

## Book Review

*Santamaria's Salesman: Working for the National Catholic Rural Movement 1959–1961*

Author: Kevin Peoples
Publisher: John Garratt Publishing, 2012.
ISBN 9781921946165.
Paperback: viii + 300 pages, price: $14.95

Reviewed by: Gregory Melleuish*

There are few more controversial figures in the history of Australia than B A Santamaria. He has had his advocates and his detractors, and books continue to be written about him, the most recent being a biography by Gerard Henderson. The most difficult task is forming a balanced assessment of Santamaria's life and work. To his supporters he was a great man who spent his life tirelessly working for causes which were inspired by principle. For his detractors he was a Machiavellian intriguer whose major impact was to split the Labor Party, thereby ensuring that Menzies remained Prime Minister for much longer than was proper.

The great virtue of Peoples' book is that it provides the perspective of one who was, for a time, an insider to the Santamaria project but who left disillusioned with the way that project was moving. It is a combination of autobiography and history as Peoples weaves his own story into that of the Santamaria organisation.

Autobiography is always difficult to interpret, especially those autobiographies written by older men and women about events which happened some decades previously. Certainly Santamaria's own autobiography needs to be read very carefully as it is very much an

---

*Gregory Melleuish is the author of *Cultural Liberalism in Australia*, *Australian Intellectuals* and other books.

apology for what he had done. Peoples' book also needs to be read with a certain care.

That said, the most vibrant parts of the book are the early chapters in which he evokes what it meant to be poor working class Catholic in rural Victoria in the 1940s. He provides a vivid picture of his family and how they coped with the vicissitudes of such a life in a dignified fashion. He tells us how dreadful his education was. And he marvels when he discovers the possibility of a tiled bathroom in the 1950s.

One can appreciate why Peoples jumped at the opportunity to become 'Santamaria's Salesman' and drive around Victoria in a new blue car extracting extra money out of members of the National Catholic Rural Movement. It gave him an independence which he could not otherwise have had. He was remarkably good at getting the farmers who he approached to part with the extra funds which the organisation required. The young man was a success.

The problem was that Peoples never quite agreed with what Santamaria was doing. He had his own views on the proper role and function of Catholic Action, ones which ultimately would place him at odds with Santamaria. While he was proud of his capacities as a salesman he was also concerned about what he was doing.

Peoples was a child of the Australian bush and his sympathies lay with country people and with their needs and wishes. The problem, for him, was that Santamaria was a city person who had no real appreciation of what it meant to live a rural existence in Australia. In his autobiography, Santamaria admits this was the case. However, this did not stop Santamaria from imposing his highly ideological views on the nature of rural life onto the members of the NCRM.

Santamaria had the old vision of an Australian countryside dotted with villages composed, hopefully of Catholic inhabitants. The full-blown utopia is to be found in Denys Jackson's 1947 work *Australian Dream, a journey to Merrion*. It was a vision of rural life in which individual farmers were largely self-sufficient rather than practising commercial farming. It was not a uniquely Catholic ideal, the idea of 'closer settlement' and of villages composed of Virtuous yeomen and their families, can be found in earlier Protestant writers, but it was seen by Santamaria as a means of ensuring the flourishing of the Faith.

For Peoples it was simply an ideology created by a city based elite that took no account of the realities of rural life. Even worse, once promulgated in the early 1940s it did not seem to change in the 1950s as conditions improved for the farmers who simply wanted an improvement in their way of life. The problem seems to have been Santamaria's implacable opposition to commercial operations and his sentimental attachment to a vision of a rural idyll. In many ways there is a great irony in Peoples' perceptive analysis as Santamaria would himself invoke the idea that he was speaking on behalf of the people against the 'elites' in coming decades.

The problem was that while Santamaria's vision held some attraction in the 1940s when rural life was harsh, by the 1950s it had lost much of its cachet for farmers who accepted the commercial realities of life on the land in Australia, something Santamaria never understood. In fact, by the late 1950s the NCRM was a shrinking organisation, boosted only by Peoples' capacity to extract funds out of its members.

This created a second problem for Peoples. He strongly suspected that the funds he raised were not being used for the benefit of farmers but to bolster other parts of the Santamaria organisation, specifically the fight against Communism, which loomed large in Santamaria's view of the world. The reality seems to have been that, by the late 1950s, the network of organisations run by Santamaria was in some trouble. He had failed to 'permeate' the ALP some years earlier leading to the creation of the Democratic Labor Party which had, as its major function, keeping the Labor Party out of office. He had lost his battles within the Church leading to the creation of the National Civic Council. And he was still only in his mid-forties.

But this did not mean that it was possible to challenge Santamaria, as Peoples discovered. Santamaria was a very charismatic man and he retained the support of a significant group of people who looked to Bob as a great leader.

The book leads to a sort of showdown at La Verna in April 1961 where Peoples ends up resigning as National Organising Secretary of the NCRM. It had clearly been two dramatic and defining years in his life. He was young and somewhat naïve but undoubtedly driven by principle. Kevin Peoples has written a fascinating book which deserves to be read for the picture which he provides for us of life within the world created by Bob Santamaria. In so doing he gives the reader an insight into a way of life which for twenty-first century Australians is now lost.

# Book Review

*Swifty: A life of Yvonne Swift*

Author: Edmund Campion
Publisher: NewSouth Publishing, Sydney, 2016
ISBN: 9781742234755
Hardback: 124 pages; price $35.00

Reviewed by Helen Scanlon*

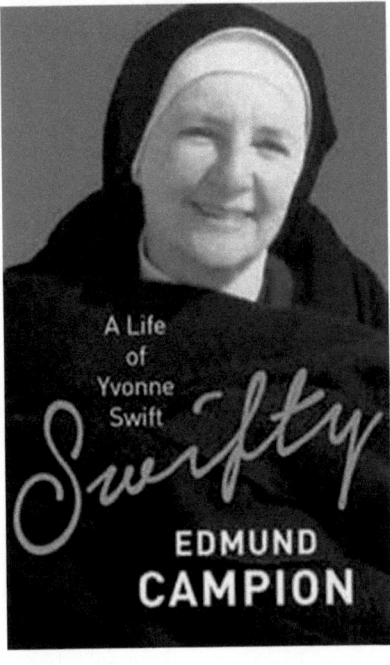

I did not have the privilege of meeting Mother Yvonne Swift in any of her roles as teacher, Principal of Sancta Sophia College or as lawyer, but having read the excellent compact biography by Edmund Campion, I can understand why she was so appreciated by her students and legal clients.

The book is well researched, each chapter dealing with a particular period of her life. It includes extensive reminiscences of those who knew her - her students, friends and associates.

Her passion for justice is traced back to her early years at Sacre Coeur School in Bourke Street, Melbourne, during the Great Depression of the 1920s. On completing her schooling, Yvonne studied Law at Melbourne University, a very male dominated faculty at that time. The tall, elegant Miss Swift was often featured in the social pages of the *Argus*, attending balls and weddings.

Yvonne graduated in 1935 but only worked as a lawyer for a few years. In 1938 she entered the Sacre Coeur Convent in Rose Bay, Sydney, where she learned to be a nun and a teacher. She qualified to teach both primary

---

* Helen Scanlon attended Sydney University 1953-6, was influenced there by university chaplain Roger Pryke and attended Newman Graduate summer schools at Sancta Sophia in the early 60s. She is secretary of the ACHS.

and secondary students, specialising in English and History. In 1948 she was made Principal of Rose Bay College in charge of 150 boarders.

In 1958 Yvonne became Principal of Sancta Sophia College, the Catholic residential college within the grounds of Sydney University. It was in this role that she became known to a wider public. Her influence after Vatican II, often working with the University Chaplain, Fr Roger Pryke, was significant. Conferences for nuns from differing orders were held at Sancta, where participants had the opportunity to study contemporary theology. She also became known to ABC radio listeners through broadcasts on the programme *Daily Devotional*.

During her time at Sancta Sophia, the universities began their expansion, so Sancta undertook a building programme to accommodate more residents. This was also a time when the Newman Association of Catholic Graduates was very active. Campion details these fruitful years when Mother Swift enabled this organisation to hold its Summer Schools at Sancta.

To satisfy her own intellectual hunger, *Swifty* took classes in the Arts Faculty of Sydney University in Latin, Greek and Hebrew, the languages of scripture. She started a scripture study group for Sancta students and introduced frequent paraliturgies. Sancta also produced its own hymn book which included Australian hymns.

*Swifty* continued to work closely with Roger Pryke; both were censured for their progressive approach by Bishop Thomas Muldoon, a very conservative and outspoken critic. Swifty also fostered a closer relationship with St John's College for Catholic men.

After many years as an educator, *Swifty* returned to the law. She took refresher courses in legal subjects at the University of NSW, and in 1973 was admitted as a solicitor of the NSW Supreme Court. She became one of just 110 female lawyers from a total of 4600. She set aside her nun's habit, dressed fashionably and was known as Miss Swift. She worked for several city firms before opening her own office in Chippendale, not far from Sydney University. She specialised initially in Family Law but soon took on criminal cases, determined to seek justice for her clients.

In 1996, aged 84 and still practising Law, *Swifty* celebrated the 50th anniversary of taking her final vows as a nun. A few years later she retired and moved to a hostel for elderly nuns. She died in 2012.

This small volume comprises 124 pages, 12 chapters and a comprehensive index. Each chapter concludes with a page or two of personal recollection by those who knew her. There are eight pages of photographs from her adult life, commencing with a photo of her as a bridesmaid and concluding with one taken in her office in Chippendale in 1992.

Campion presents us with a portrait of a remarkable woman religious who lived a full and varied life in a century of great social, religious and cultural change. Readers who lived through the post Vatican II years in Sydney will particularly enjoy being reminded of those eventful times.

## Book Review

*A Listening Ministry: Becoming a Bishop in Our World*

Author: Archbishop Leonard Faulkner
Editor: Father Michael Trainor
Publishers: Morning Star Publishing, Northcote, Vic
ISBN: 9780994470713
Paperback: 145 pages, price: $20

Book review by Michael Costigan*

Some of Australia's better known bishops, like Daniel Mannix, Patrick Moran, James Duhig, Thomas Carr, Matthew Beovich and George Pell, have been the subjects of mostly fine biographies. Few, however, have written their own life stories, offering posterity unique insights into their own backgrounds, activities, views, achievements, failures and spiritual journeys.

That is one of a number of reasons why this memoir by the former Archbishop of Adelaide, recently turned ninety and living in retirement, deserves a hearty welcome.

Leonard Faulkner, born in late 1926, was raised in the sparsely populated countryside in South Australia's Mid North, close to the foothills of the Flinders Ranges. He became in turn an Adelaide diocesan priest (1950-66), Bishop of Townsville (1967-83), Coadjutor (1983-85) and then Archbishop (1985-2001) of Adelaide. His mainly chronological account of every stage in his long life was inspired by the Adelaide priest Michael Trainor, who,

---

\* Michael Costigan was Associate Editor of *The Advocate* (Melbourne); founding Director of the Literature Board of the Australia Council; and first Executive Secretary of the Australian Bishops Committee for Justice, Development and Peace. He is an Adjunct Professor of Australian Catholic University.

over two years, taped and transcribed into text a series of life-probing interviews with the elderly but still mentally agile prelate.

The result of this diligent act of devotion is a charming and instructive volume in which the wise and gentle voice of "this thoroughly open and great Australian bishop", as Trainor calls him, is unmistakenly audible.

Most of Len Faulkner's reminiscences are positive. His childhood in several small country towns and settlements, as the eldest in a large and at times financially straitened family, involved hardships, but his memories of those distant days in the late 1920s and the 1930s are not unhappy. The influence of his devoutly religious parents, of Josephite teachers and of country priests in what is now the Port Pirie Diocese (until 1951 it was Port Augusta) clearly stayed with him for the rest of his life. And the responsibilities given to him in the family helped to form the character and style of one who was usually given leadership roles at most stages in his later life.

By the 1940s, the teenager and afterwards his whole family had moved to Adelaide, where his education continued under the Marist Brothers at Sacred Heart College and, in 1942, at the age of sixteen, as one of the first group of minor seminarians at St Francis Xavier's, Rostrevor, newly created by Atchbishop Beovich.

The Archbishop then sent the promising young priesthood aspirant to Corpus Christi College, Werribee (1943-46) and on to Beovich's own much loved alma mater, Propaganda Fide College, Rome (1946-50), where Faulkner was ordained on New Year's Day 1950.

The chapters on his two major seminaries are of special interest at a time when the positives and above all the negatives of priests' training in the past are under scrutiny. Again, Archbishop Faulkner gives more attention to the system's virtues, as he experienced them, than to its defects. He values in particular the form of spirituality conveyed to their charges by the Jesuits at Werribee and the pastoral training provided by superiors like Fathers Henry Johnston SJ and Charles Mayne SJ. He found the spiritual directorship available at Propaganda not so impressive, although the example given by a saintly Rector, Monsignor Felice Cenci, helped to compensate for that.

In both seminaries he took on board the approach, principles and pastoral methodology advocated by the Young Christian Workers (Jocist) movement and its world leader, the Belgian Monsignor (later Cardinal) Joseph Cardijn, who liked to visit and stay in touch with potential Church leaders among Propaganda Fide's students. This was to be significant in Faulkner's ministry as a priest and bishop. Clerics who imbibed Jocist spirituality were to be among those best prepared to understand and apply in their work the spirit and teaching of Vatican II. Len Faulkner was one of them.

The part played by the Council in Faulkner's ministry is manifest from his own recollections of his clerical career.

As a young priest working as a curate in Woodville and for a time as the Diocesan Chaplain for the YCW, he, like the rest of the Church, was unaware that a Pope soon to be elected, John XXIII, would convene the Council, but he was already prepared for what were to become its vital lessons about the need for the clergy to encourage dialogue and to be listeners as well as teachers.

During the second half of his next assignment, as Administrator of Adelaide's Cathedral, the Council was taking place and he had the key role of assisting Archbishops Beovich and James Gleeson, returning from Rome after each of its four annual sessions (1962-65), to present its good news to "the People of God".

Then, in 1967, came the 41-year-old priest's ordination as Bishop of Townsville. A surprise appointment to a diocese he had never visited, it came less than two years after the Council ended. It gave the new appointee the opportunity, accepted with at least a degree of success, to set an example as a bishop intent on applying the Council's teachings and decisions.

The Archbishop is modest in his own assessment of his years in Northern Queensland. He writes (page 101): "I was very happy in those sixteen years. I thank God for the opportunity to live and work with these great people spread across a thousand miles. I think about the effort I put in to bring about the Diocesan Pastoral Council and parish councils. This was possibly the most effective part of my ministry because it involved wonderful lay people, men and women, young men and women too."

From the beginning the new Bishop made it his business to meet and learn from the large communities of Aboriginal and Islander people in his diocese. In the end, however, he considered he was unsuccessful "in the sense that they did not take a leading part in the life of the Diocese". He was consoled, however, to find after leaving, on a return visit to Townsville, that some First Australians were by then taking leadership and doing much for the Church, especially in Mount Isa.

Writing of his return to Adelaide in a Church leadership role, the Archbishop reveals the kind of pride that Catholics in the South Australian capital often display in the achievements of their Church. He claims that "Adelaide was one of the best dioceses prepared for the Second Vatican Council"; that "it received the Council well"; and that "the spirit of the Council was absorbed into the Diocese – it was initially set up by Archbishop Beovich, developed by Jim Gleeson in his way and I tried to make my contribution to this in my time, too".

After a period of careful planning and consultation, that contribution in Adelaide notably included the innovative creation of a Diocesan Pastoral Team. Its four-person membership included initially Faulkner himself, his Vicar-General, a female Religious and a laywoman. One of the more significant and fruitful tasks of the Team became parish visitation, which in most dioceses has always been primarily a bishop's responsibility. The Team also gave priority to ecumenism and hospitality. So successful was the Team idea that Faulkner is surprised that other bishops have not followed suit.

In Adelaide, as in Townsville, the Archbishop gave a high priority to the Vatican Council's emphasis on dialogue, inter-church relations, the role of the laity and social justice. Cardijn's inductive "see, judge and act" methodology was central to his understanding of today's episcopal ministry, which also required that the diocesan leader should be above all a listener, as the title chosen for the memoir underlines.

In all of this, Faulkner was helped in Adelaide by advisers like the theologian Father Denis Edwards, long-time priest-friends Ted Mulvihill, Gavan Kennare and James O'Loughlin and such lay activists as the ex-seminarian David Shinnick.

He did not find that the pastoral approach of organisations like *Opus Dei* and the *Neo-Catechumenate* quite met his aspirations. Hence, in spite of his esteem for their qualities, he resisted pressure to invite them to be his collaborators.

While Len Faulkner has mainly positive recollections of his time in both Townsville and Adelaide, he admits to what he sees as certain of his failures and disappointments. The departures of a number of priests from their calling caused him much sadness. And he does not hesitate to castigate those Vatican authorities who refused permission for his diocese to continue using what had been the pastorally beneficial and popular Third Rite of Reconciliation. In this he was at one with Bishop William Morris, whose tenure as head of the Toowoomba Diocese was so unjustifiably terminated in 2011.

Personally, I have reason to be grateful to the Archbishop for the part he played, with the late Cardinal Clancy, in making successful representations to Cardinal Ratzinger over the criticism of the Australian Bishops by that future Pope's Congregation for the Doctrine of the Faith for appointing one who had left the active priesthood, myself, to a key position in the Bishops Conference's bureaucracy. Faulkner pays tribute to Cardinal Clancy (page 128) for persuading such a powerful member of the Roman Curia that no action should be taken over the appointment, which was to continue for many years after the controversy was settled in my favour.

Although Len Faulkner does not expand on the background to this episode, I had more to say in public last year about the conflict and the role believed to have been played in it by the Pro-Nuncio to Australia, the late Archbishop Franco Brambilla. This was in a paper delivered in September 2016 to the Fiftieth Annual Conference of the Canon Law Society of Australia and New Zealand ("Reminiscences of a Founding Father: Church, Law and Social Justice" by Dr Michael Costigan JUD, STL, Proceedings, pages 66-68).

Some readers of *A Listening Ministry* may find it repetitious at times and may think that a few of the Archbishop's asides could have been edited out. For me, however, one of the book's delights is that it reads exactly for what it is – the taped reminiscences of an elderly man, presented much as it was spoken in a series of long sessions while he looked back over a long life of achievement. Most importantly, it is a faithful record of the life of one of Australia's most outstanding Vatican II bishops.

If a second edition of the memoir is contemplated, one hopes that a number of incorrect spellings will be corrected. They include the surnames of Cardinals Joseph Bernardin and Pietro Parente, Archbishop Justin Simonds, Bishop John Satterthwaite and Father Henry Johnston SJ; the first names of Archbishop Guilford Young and Mr Denys Jackson; the Latin name of Propaganda Fide College; and the place name of Castelgandolfo, where Propaganda College's summer villa (alongside the papal villa) existed in Len Faulkner's and the present reviewer's (slightly later) days as Roman seminarians.

These suggestions do not detract from the gratitude owed to Father Trainor for thinking of this valuable publication and, with his helpers, for making its production possible.

## Book Review

*Beyond Belief*

Author: Hugh Mackay
Editor: Father Michael Trainor
Publishers: Macmillan, Australia
ISBN: 9781743534854
Paperback: 280 pages, price: $32.99

Reviewed by Roy Williams*

Australian social commentator Hugh Mackay describes his latest book, *Beyond Belief*, as one "for doubters, sceptics, heretics, agnostics and religious fringe-dwellers". He explicitly cautions "committed Christians" and "committed atheists" that it is "not likely to appeal".

Although I am an orthodox (Protestant) Christian, Mackay's warning, delivered at the book's outset, did not faze me. Nor his honest confession that his expertise is as a social psychologist and researcher, not a theologian. Several books by self-confessed agnostics and atheists were crucial in my own path to faith – they got me thinking, probably in ways unintended by their authors.

Reading this book, however, was a frustrating experience. The chief reason is that Mackay is not the agnostic he says he is. In his own urbane way, he is as closed-minded as many of the religious and irreligious zealots whom, often justly, he attacks.

The idea of "faith" which Mackay extols – humanism, really, with respect for Jesus' moral teachings – excludes *as a matter of course* any element of the supernatural. Mackay thus falls into the very trap that he himself identifies:

We impose our own values, preconceptions and expectations on what

---

*Roy Williams was an agnostic until the age of 35. He is now a Christian author. His most recent book is *Post-God Nation?*

we see and interpret it accordingly: the viewer is always part of the view. From then on, we will tend to process any relevant information *selectively*, being especially attentive to messages that confirm the information we have previously taken on board. Conversely, we'll be less inclined to attend to messages that challenge or contradict it. (original emphasis)

I will return to this theme, but first it is appropriate to recognise the valuable elements of *Beyond Belief*. There are several.

For a start, Mackay appreciates that religious faith has always brought priceless benefits to the world – not least a sense of meaning and purpose for literally billions of individual believers. He points out that there is nothing "irrational" in the human impulses to be taken seriously and to connect with others, and to give and receive love.

The book also contains excerpts from interviews conducted by Mackay with ordinary Australians about their religious beliefs (or lack thereof). These are always fascinating, if frequently worrying and sad – at least for anyone who cares about the Church.

To give the flavour, here are the musings of a youngish married father named Richard:

> I'm actually a believer, sort of. I mean, I'm certainly not an atheist. I was raised a Catholic, and I want my kids to have that upbringing too. But the thing is, going to church is a two-and-a-half hour exercise ... If we have any spare time as a family, we're inclined to have a walk by the water, get some fresh air, buy fish and chips and have a bit of family time together. *I'd give up church before I'd give that up.* (my emphasis)

Another strength of Mackay's book is the analysis of two important social phenomena, prevalent both in Australia and across the West – the existence of millions of people who confess to "faith envy" and/or who identify as "Spiritual But Not Religious".

Mackay has conversed with many such people. Variously they yearn to believe in something beyond themselves; they admire other people who live by faith, but cannot adhere to any formalised "dogma" or "creed". According to Mackay these "seekers" are the products of reaction against neo-liberal materialism and institutionalised religion. Some wear the SBNR label like "a badge of authenticity".

One interviewee describes the mindset thus: "it's vaguely pantheistic, mixed with the need for kindness – some sort of sixties-hippie, with some Buddhism thrown in ... by doing good, you'll become good".

All this is worthwhile stuff – as social research and observation. It is when Mackay dips into Christian theology that the book becomes irritating. More than that – it is emblematic of the tragic religious and scientific ignorance of most modern-day Australians.

Mackay professes to be a "Christian agnostic". He urges tolerance of all faiths. Yet the following passage (and numerous others like it) left me exasperated:

[W]hen the central myths of the Christian tradition – virgin birth, resurrection, miracles – are presented as historical rather than metaphorical truths, Christian apologists tie themselves in all kinds of knots. If you're going to argue that such things actually happened, you will run into a wall of scientific and other resistance. On the other hand, if you embrace such stories as seminal myths, rich with meaning and redolent with wisdom, the resistance crumbles; who's going to argue with the underlying truth, the inner meaning, of a myth?

Then the kicker:

It would be as absurd to deny the value to our culture of the Christian myths as it would be to try to defend them as historical fact.

So Mackay dismisses as "absurd" – self-evidently so – all supernatural aspects of the Christian (and presumably any other) faith. In support of this presupposition he cites "modern theological scholarship", referring periodically to the likes of Paul Tilloch, Hugh Schonfield, John A T Robinson, John Shelby Spong, John Dominic Crossan and A N Wilson.

It might be observed that these are scarcely "modern" sources. Tilloch's most influential books were written in the 1950s; Schonfield's and Robinson's in the 1960s. The heydays of J D Crossan and Bishop Spong came in the 1980s and 90s. (A N Wilson, moreover, is no longer an atheist – he re-converted a few years ago, swearing publicly that "I shall never make the same mistake again".)

More to the point, all of these men – including Wilson during his atheist phase – were, and are, representative of a *tiny* minority among Christian commentators. Their work must be understood in proper context.

Mackay is obviously an empathetic and intelligent man. I would urge him to read some mainstream, world-class theology written in the twenty-first century. Say, N.T. Wright on the Resurrection. Or Hugh Ross on Christianity and modern science. Or Paul K. Moser on the nature of religious knowledge. Any recent Papal encyclical. He may find his own beliefs are challenged.

# SANTAMARIA'S SALESMAN

### WORKING FOR THE
### NATIONAL CATHOLIC RURAL MOVEMENT
### 1959—1961

**KEVIN PEOPLES**

'Gerard Henderson has done Australian history a considerable service with this hugely ambitious biography.'
GERALDINE DOOGUE

# SANTAMARIA
*A Most Unusual Man*

# GERARD HENDERSON

Printed by Libri Plureos GmbH in Hamburg, Germany